New Directions for Teaching and Learning

Catherine M. Wehlburg
EDITOR-IN-CHIEF

D1279365

Evidence-Based Teaching

William Buskist
James E. Groccia
EDITORS

Number 128 • Winter 2011
Jossey-Bass
San Francisco

EVIDENCE-BASED TEACHING
William Buskist, James E. Groccia (eds.)
New Directions for Teaching and Learning, no. 128
Catherine M. Wehlburg, Editor-in-Chief

Copyright © 2011 Wiley Periodicals, Inc., A Wiley Company. All rights reserved. No part of this publication may be reproduced, stored in a retrieval system, or transmitted in any form or by any means, electronic, mechanical, photocopying, recording, scanning, or otherwise, except as permitted under Section 107 or 108 of the 1976 United States Copyright Act, without either the prior written permission of the Publisher or authorization through payment of the appropriate per-copy fee to the Copyright Clearance Center, 222 Rosewood Drive, Danvers, MA 01923, (978) 750-8400, fax (978) 646-8600. Requests to the Publisher for permission should be addressed to the Permissions Department, c/o John Wiley & Sons, Inc., 111 River St., Hoboken, NJ 07030; (201) 748-8789, fax (201) 748-6326, http://www.wiley.com/go/permissions.

Microfilm copies of issues and articles are available in 16mm and 35mm, as well as microfiche in 105mm, through University Microfilms, Inc., 300 North Zeeb Road, Ann Arbor, MI 48106-1346.

NEW DIRECTIONS FOR TEACHING AND LEARNING (ISSN 0271-0633, electronic ISSN 1536-0768) is part of The Jossey-Bass Higher and Adult Education Series and is published quarterly by Wiley Subscription Services, Inc., A Wiley Company, at Jossey-Bass, One Montgomery Street, Suite 1200, San Francisco, CA 94104-4594. Periodicals postage paid at San Francisco, CA, and at additional mailing offices. POSTMASTER: Send address changes to New Directions for Teaching and Learning, Jossey-Bass, One Montgomery Street, Suite 1200, San Francisco, CA 94104-4594.

New Directions for Teaching and Learning is indexed in CIJE: Current Index to Journals in Education (ERIC), Contents Pages in Education (T&F), Current Abstracts (EBSCO), Educational Research Abstracts Online (T&F), ERIC Database (Education Resources Information Center), Higher Education Abstracts (Claremont Graduate University), and SCOPUS (Elsevier).

SUBSCRIPTIONS cost $89 for individuals and $275 for institutions, agencies, and libraries in the United States. Prices subject to change.

EDITORIAL CORRESPONDENCE should be sent to the editor-in-chief, Catherine M. Wehlburg, c.wehlburg@tcu.edu.

www.josseybass.com

CONTENTS

Editors' Notes   1
William Buskist, James E. Groccia

1. Need for Evidence-Based Teaching   5
James E. Groccia, William Buskist
This chapter describes what evidence-based teaching is and why it is
necessary for enhancing the quality of teaching and learning that takes
place in higher education, thus providing a rationale for the remaining
chapters in the volume.

2. The Lecture   13
S. Raj Chaudhury
This chapter reviews the basic mechanics of the lecture and describes
the variety of ways that approaches to lecturing might be enhanced
based on recent research advances in the cognitive sciences.

3. Problem-Based Learning   21
Deborah E. Allen, Richard S. Donham, Stephen A. Bernhardt
The authors describe the fundamental components of problem-based
learning and review the research data on its effectiveness as a teaching
tool for fostering deep student learning.

4. Case Study Teaching   31
Clyde Freeman Herreid
This chapter outlines the variety of case study teaching methods, the
conditions under which teachers most often use them and its effectiveness in producing student learning. In addition, the author describes a
model to help teachers decide which case study method to use given
their particular teaching and learning goals.

5. Team-Based Learning   41
Larry K. Michaelsen, Michael Sweet
The authors explain the principles on which team-based learning is
predicated and the value of this system in promoting team development and critical thinking. This chapter also reviews the empirical evidence for the effectiveness of team-based learning in producing deep
student learning.

6. Interteaching   53
Bryan K. Saville, Tracy E. Zinn
Drawing on the early history of behavioral approaches to higher education, the authors describe a relatively new teaching system called interteaching and review the growing body of evidence of its effectiveness
relative to traditional approaches to college and university teaching.

7. Just-in-Time Teaching   63

Gregor M. Novak

This chapter details the nuts and bolts of Just-in-Time Teaching and the implementation procedures for using it in the college classroom. The author also reviews research evidence showing that this system of teaching enhances student motivation and deep learning.

8. Service-Learning   75

Peter Felten, Patti H. Clayton

Focusing on the unique ways in which service-learning engages students in learning, the authors elucidate the basic principles underlying this system of teaching and learning and evaluate the evidence that it enhances student learning outcomes across a variety of outcomes, including transformative learning.

9. Web-Based Computer-Aided Personalized System of Instruction   85

Joseph J. Pear, Gabriel J. Schnerch, Kathleen M. Silva, Louis Svenningsen, Jody Lambert

This chapter describes a Web-based approach to teaching and learning known as Computer-Aided Personalized System of Instruction. The authors review its basic tenets, the means by which it is implemented, and the evidence supporting its effectiveness in achieving high rates of student learning.

10. Online Learning   95

Edward H. Perry, Michelle L. Pilati

The authors trace the history of online teaching, review its basic principles and methods of implementation, address faculty resistance to it, and evaluate its effectiveness for producing positive student learning outcomes.

11. Evidence-Based Teaching: Now and in the Future   105

William Buskist, James E. Groccia

This chapter reviews the basic empirical findings supporting each of the teaching and learning systems described in earlier chapters and calls for a concerted effort on the part of all teachers to expand the evidence base of effective college and university teaching.

INDEX   113

FROM THE SERIES EDITOR

About This Publication

Since 1980, *New Directions for Teaching and Learning (NDTL)* has brought a unique blend of theory, research, and practice to leaders in postsecondary education. *NDTL* sourcebooks strive not only for solid substance but also for timeliness, compactness, and accessibility.

The series has four goals: to inform readers about current and future directions in teaching and learning in postsecondary education, to illuminate the context that shapes these new directions, to illustrate these new directions through examples from real settings, and to propose ways in which these new directions can be incorporated into still other settings.

This publication reflects the view that teaching deserves respect as a high form of scholarship. We believe that significant scholarship is conducted not only by researchers who report results of empirical investigations but also by practitioners who share disciplinary reflections about teaching. Contributors to *NDTL* approach questions of teaching and learning as seriously as they approach substantive questions in their own disciplines, and they deal not only with pedagogical issues, but also with the intellectual and social context in which these issues arise. Authors deal on the one hand with theory and research and on the other with practice, and they translate from research and theory to practice and back again.

About This Volume

In some ways, there has been a great deal of research done on teaching and learning. However, there is still much that we don't know. There may not be a "best" teaching practice or the "right" way to learn. So many variables interact during the teaching and learning process that it is very difficult to make sense of the vast amount of research and opinion on how to teach. There is so much information, perhaps, that it is easy to become overwhelmed and just teach the way we were taught. Evidence-based teaching is an important way to approach what we know about teaching and learning and how to tease through the vast amount of information to decide on what to use. This volume encourages using evidence and research-supported practices to develop a new tradition of teaching.

Catherine M. Wehlburg
Editor-in-Chief

CATHERINE M. WEHLBURG *is the assistant provost for Institutional Effectiveness at Texas Christian University.*

EDITORS' NOTES

Although college and university teachers have long emphasized effective teaching (e.g., James, [1899] 1962), the last two decades have witnessed an especially powerful upsurge in empirical research on investigating what it means to teach effectively (for example, Bain, 2004; Gurung and Schwartz, 2009; Lowman, 1995). This trend was likely prompted by the convergence of two important events: the publication of Ernst Boyer's (1990) now-classic *Scholarship Reconsidered*, which ignited the SoTL (scholarship of teaching and learning) "movement," and the national call for teachers at all levels to become more accountable for the effectiveness of their teaching methods. The result of this outpouring of pedagogical research is the building of a firm evidence base for many teaching practices. Indeed, disciplinary-specific pedagogical journals as well as more general teaching journals are flourishing and new ones have appeared (for example, the *International Journal for the Scholarship of Teaching and Learning*); teaching conferences or research conferences with teaching programs embedded within them are as popular as ever; and teaching and learning centers, which exist primarily to improve teaching effectiveness, are now the keystone feature of faculty development on hundreds of college and university campuses.

SoTL exists in many forms, but for our purposes, we have conceptualized it as having primarily only two. One form is research that is conducted on discrete aspects of teaching—those techniques and tactics that can be dropped into a course at any point during the semester and at the teacher's will, such as demonstrations, discussion questions, classroom assessment techniques, and so on. The research question of course is always the same: Will this technique or tactic improve students' learning of concept X? The defining feature of this sort of SoTL is that the research is conducted on only one unique aspect of the class. A glance at any pedagogical journal will reveal that this research constitutes a substantial proportion of SoTL work.

The other form of SoTL has been the development and refinement of "systems" of teaching and learning that define how a course is taught throughout the semester. This sort of research aims at identifying not only the system's effectiveness at achieving high student learning outcomes throughout the course but also the key components of it that are responsible for this achievement. Among the earliest, and indeed the classic example, of such systems is Keller's (1968) personalized system of instruction (PSI) in which a given course is structured, from beginning to end, in a format that strictly defines both the teacher's role in facilitating learning

NEW DIRECTIONS FOR TEACHING AND LEARNING, no. 128, Winter 2011 © Wiley Periodicals, Inc.
Published online in Wiley Online Library (wileyonlinelibrary.com) • DOI: 10.1002/tl.462

and the student's role in interacting with that information and exhibiting the extent to which it is learned.

Since Keller's original research, a variety of systems of teaching and learning have emerged. This volume of *New Directions for Teaching and Learning* focuses on these systems for two reasons. The first is to introduce readers to the array of such evidence-based systems that are currently in practice in many colleges and universities, thus providing an accessible resource to support instructional efforts and inform and improve teaching practices. The second is to summarize the empirical evidence that reinforces the effectiveness of some of these systems.

We began this project after many years of work to enhance teaching and learning processes in our individual instructional practices and with graduate students and faculty members in faculty development settings. After reviewing the data, we strongly believe that several evidence-based systems of teaching and learning can be used in a variety of different instructional settings, depending on one's teaching goals and student learning objectives.

Accordingly, there are two primary audiences for this volume. The first is graduate students, postdoctoral fellows, full- and part-time faculty members, tenure track and non–tenure track instructors—in short, anyone providing instruction to students within a higher education context. The second is faculty developers—those academic professionals responsible for assisting instructional staff in providing high-quality learning experiences for their students. Both of these audiences will likely benefit from having a concise and clear resource for understanding, implementing, and revising contextually appropriate systems of teaching and learning.

In addition to serving as a compendium of the latest research and theory on evidence-based teaching (EBT), this volume also provides a rationale for adopting EBT practices as well as the need for continued empirical investigation to provide richer and broader evidence of teaching effectiveness. We provide ten examples of evidence-based systems of teaching and learning, including the lecture, in this volume. Our coverage of systems of teaching is not exhaustive; rather it is representative of the kinds of systems of teaching and learning currently in practice. Our authors are expert practitioners who invented and developed a particular system or who are leading researchers into a specific system. In general, each article adheres to the same format, starting with an introduction to the system, followed with advice on how to implement it, and concluding with a summary of the evidence that supports the effectiveness of that system relative to student learning and student enjoyment of learning.

As you read and think about the contents of this volume, keep in mind that every system of teaching and learning may be applicable to a range of instructional settings, but not likely all of them. Thus, in thinking about how well a particular system may work for you as a teacher, be mindful of the particular instructional context in which you teach. It is also important for you to think carefully about what sort of modifications you could make to tweak or otherwise tinker with a given system so that you could implement it for your purposes. In that way, you, too, can participate in, and contribute to, the growing body of literature on EBT.

William Buskist
James E. Groccia
Editors

References

Bain, K. *What the Best College Teachers Do*. Cambridge, Mass.: Harvard University Press, 2004.

Boyer, E. L. *Scholarship Reconsidered: Priorities of the Professoriate*. New York: Carnegie Foundation for the Advancement of Teaching, 1990.

Gurung, R.A.R., and Schwartz, B. M. *Optimizing Teaching and Learning: Practicing Pedagogical Research*. Malden, Mass.: Wiley-Blackwell, 2009.

James, W. *Talks to Teachers on Psychology and to Students on Some of Life's Ideals*. Mineola, N.Y.: Dover, 1962. (Originally published 1899.)

Keller, F. S. "Good-bye, Teacher . . ." *Journal of Applied Behavior Analysis*, 1968, *1*, 79–89.

Lowman, J. *Mastering the Techniques of Teaching*. (2nd ed.) San Francisco: Jossey-Bass, 1995.

WILLIAM BUSKIST *is the distinguished professor in the teaching of psychology and a faculty fellow at the Biggio Center for the Enhancement of Teaching and Learning at Auburn University.*

JAMES E. GROCCIA *is director of the Biggio Center for the Enhancement of Teaching and Learning and associate professor of higher education at Auburn University.*

This chapter reviews the current status of university teaching and provides an overview for the need for evidence-based teaching. It describes problems with defining evidence as well as distinctions among systems of teaching and specific teaching actions.

Need for Evidence-Based Teaching

James E. Groccia, William Buskist

Teaching is just too damned difficult to get right. It is always possible to improve.

—Petty, 2006, p. ix

Petty's words send a clarion message to college and university teachers around the world. However, we believe that rather than being a mere possibility to improve as teachers, it is always *necessary* to improve. One way of improving our teaching is to adopt teaching methods that are based on or supported by evidence of success in enhancing student learning.

Current Status of Higher Education: Critics and Supporters

Most teachers base their instructional practices on tradition, the opinion of experienced practitioners, ideology, faddism, marketing, politics, or personal experience gained through trial and error (Beder and Medina, 2001; Slavin, 2008). This volume presents several of what we call evidence-based systems of teaching. We encourage readers to look at the evidence supporting each system and consider if one or more of these instructional approaches would help them achieve their teaching and student learning objectives. We hope that this volume will help develop a new tradition of teaching—one based on evidence and research-supported practice.

Some faculty may see evidence-based teaching (EBT) as the latest fad in education, but we believe that it is more than a new trendy fashion. It refers to an approach that holds that practice should be capable of being

NEW DIRECTIONS FOR TEACHING AND LEARNING, no. 128, Winter 2011 © Wiley Periodicals, Inc.
Published online in Wiley Online Library (wileyonlinelibrary.com) • DOI: 10.1002/tl.463

justified in terms of sound evidence about its likely outcomes. As Robert Cole (1999) stated: "Education may not be an exact science, but it is too important to allow it to be determined by unfounded opinion, whether of politicians, teachers, researchers, or anyone else" (p. 1). Yet it is ironic that within higher education institutions dedicated to the discovery, transformation, and dissemination of knowledge, the choice of teaching strategies is based largely on experiential, commonsense, or anecdotal evidence.

In recent years, there have been calls for education to follow the fields of medicine and agriculture and embrace evidence as a foundation for practice. These calls have resulted in several national efforts in the United States, such as No Child Left Behind, What Works Clearinghouse, Comprehensive School Reform Quality Center, and the Best Evidence Encyclopedia; the Evidence for Policy and Practice Information and Co-ordination Centre in the United Kingdom; and the Campbell Collaboration in Norway (Slavin, 2008). However, these efforts have focused on primary and secondary (K–12) education, not higher or tertiary education.

As the world continues to shrink, or become "flatter," in Thomas Friedman's (2007) terms, the quality of higher education and the need to facilitate high-level learning has never been more important. The new world economy is highly knowledge intensive, and to succeed, one must be good at constantly learning—if one stands still, one falls back (Rischard, 2002). What goes on inside the world's higher-education classrooms has a profound impact on more than an individual student's grades: Global economic and social success, and even worldwide survival, may rest in the balance (Groccia, 2010). Higher education stands at a crossroads; millions of students are entering a higher-education system that requires a recalibration of teaching methods and learning outcomes (American Association of Colleges and Universities, 2007). To be maximally relevant to this emerging new world reality, everyone involved with college and university teaching, regardless of discipline, must recognize the need to use the most effective teaching and learning methods.

Higher education, specifically its focus on quality teaching, has experienced much criticism in the past two decades. Under the general term "accountability," legislative and governing bodies as well as public interest groups increasingly ask for evidence of higher education's impact. Rightly or wrongly, parents and students appear to believe that colleges are expensive and wasteful. The public seems to be increasingly dissatisfied with higher education's perceived lack of interest in teaching due to increasing emphasis on research, publication, and disciplinary specialization, all of which seem to be largely unrelated to students' academic welfare (Bok, 2006; Boyer Commission on Educating Undergraduates in the Research University, 1998; Kline, 1977).

Despite increased curricular offerings, expansion of educational services and resources, the use of powerful educational technology, and development of innovative new curricula to meet the challenges of the twenty-first century, there is little hard evidence that our students learn more than they did fifty years ago (Bok, 2006). As a result, Bok has called for increased attention to improved teaching, more student engagement in learning, and higher quality faculty development to revitalize U.S. higher education.

The National Center for Public Policy and Higher Education (NCPPHE, 2006), in its review of worldwide educational statistics, provided evidence that U.S. higher education, when compared with educational outcomes in other countries, is not doing so well by its students. For example, in the report, the United States ranked sixteenth of twenty-seven developed countries in the percentage of students who complete their first undergraduate degree. This report clearly indicates that American higher education is underperforming relative to many other countries (NCPPHE, 2006).

The ever-increasing price of attending America's colleges and universities has also drawn increased attention with respect to whether students and their parents are getting what they paid for. According to the National Center for Educational Statistics (2007), for the 2006–2007 academic year, the net cost of attending college grew at a faster rate than both median income and disposable per capita income during the 1980s and 1990s at all types of U.S. higher-education institutions. Adding to the problem of rising costs is the added debt burden that students and parents must shoulder as they try to finance college education. According to data published by the Project on Student Debt (2010), in 2008, 67 percent of students graduating from four-year colleges and universities had student loan debt, and the average debt for a graduating senior rose to $23,200 from $18,650 in 2004 (a 24 percent increase). An even more important impact for the future is the resulting reduction in access to higher education for students with limited financial means due to increasing costs and debt.

Thus, given that college and university education is expensive and at many institutions the quality of education students receive may be questionable, it seems reasonable to ask, if not demand, that teachers modify their approaches to instruction and use the most effective teaching methods currently available. Using proven effective teaching techniques would enhance the quality of student learning and perhaps quiet critics who lament the poor preparation of students for living and working in the "real world."

Nature of Evidence-Based Teaching and Its Implications for Teaching and Learning

EBT has its roots in the clinical fields of medicine, nursing, psychology, and social work. Sackett, Rosenberg, Gray, Haynes, and Richardson (1996) defined evidence-based medicine as "integrating individual clinical expertise with the best available external clinical evidence from systematic research" (pp. 71–72). The American Psychological Association (2005) defined evidence-based practice as the "integration of the best available research with clinical expertise in the context of patient characteristics, culture, and preferences" (p. 1). Kazdin (2008) defined evidence-based treatment as "the interventions or techniques . . . that have produced therapeutic change in controlled trials" (p. 147). Based on these definitions, Metz, Espiritu, and Moore (2007) developed this definition of evidence-based practice for out-of-school educational settings: "The integration of the best available research with out-of-school time expertise within the context of child, teen, family, and community characteristics, culture, and preferences" (p. 1). Adapting these definitions to settings in higher education, we define EBT as

> the conscientious, explicit, and judicious integration of best available research on teaching technique and expertise within the context of student, teacher, department, college, university, and community characteristics.

EBT is not without controversy. Researchers and educators disagree about several critical issues, including definitions of what constitutes evidence, appropriateness of adopting medical or agricultural models for use in educational settings, the managerial agenda of evidence-based education, the role of values in educational research and practice, and the amount of accumulated knowledge necessary on which to base practice (Biesta, 2007). We do not attempt to resolve these issues here but instead take a more pragmatic, applied approach and focus on general systems of teaching that link research to practice in ways that might also be labeled evidence suggested, evidence informed, or evidence influenced.

One does not need to use a meta-analysis of all relevant randomized controlled trials to establish a definition and basis of evidence for good practice. Rating systems to assess the hierarchy of levels of evidence as espoused by others (e.g., LoBiondo-Wood and Haber, 2006) go far beyond the typical college classroom instructor's expertise and time availability. In the face of current realities of how college faculty teach and the process by which they choose their instructional approaches, any decision to adopt a particular system of teaching that considers evidence from reviews of systematic descriptive, quantitative, and qualitative studies would be a clear improvement. The teaching systems presented in this volume rest on accessible and useful evidence. Teachers can be secure in their choice of any or all of these approaches, as each has been clearly documented to be effective in enhancing student learning.

In addition to what we know about teaching, we also know a lot about how people learn (Bransford, Brown, and Cocking, 2000). Ambrose and others (2010) described seven principles of learning that underpin academic practice and form the building blocks in the construction of integrated, holistic systems of teaching. These seven principles are:

1. Prior knowledge influences current and future learning.
2. How students organize knowledge influences how they learn and how they apply what they know.
3. Motivation determines, directs, and sustains learning.
4. Students develop learning mastery by acquiring component skills and practicing combining and integrating them.
5. Goal-directed practice coupled with targeted feedback facilitates learning.
6. Emotional, social, and intellectual climate factors influence learning.
7. Metacognitive monitoring of learning facilitates further learning.

These seven evidence-based principles identify specific behaviors or conditions that influence learning, either of which in turn influence specific faculty teaching skills and techniques that can be then combined into integrated systems of teaching. However, our focus on systems of teaching does not describe the empirical evidence behind these principles of how people learn or the specific components of teaching and learning (e.g., feedback, active learning, testing effects, dual code channels) or other teaching techniques that are not part of a formalized, highly developed instructional system approach. Instead, our focus is on the integrated systems of teaching per se and their overall effectiveness in (a) producing changes in students' learning and (b) the extent to which students enjoy the process of learning. Indeed, the importance of investigating specific components of these integrated systems is a strong impetus for future research on these systems, a topic we take up in the final article in this volume.

Before we suggest that faculty members adopt EBT methods, it is useful to get a sense of current teaching approaches used in U.S. college classrooms. The most recent data reported by the Higher Education Research Institute at the University of California Los Angeles (DeAngelo and others, 2009, p. 10) on faculty approaches to teaching are presented in Table 1.

The teaching techniques highlighted in the DeAngelo et al. report, with the exception of cooperative learning and lecturing, are specific pedagogic actions, not integrated systems of teaching. According to these data, there has been a marked reduction in the use of extensive lecturing from 2005 to 2008 coupled with small increases in student-centered teaching approaches. In light of this information on how faculty members currently teach, there seems to be much room for the adoption of evidence-based teaching methods. Access to models of teaching systems based on evidence, such as those presented in this volume, should lead to higher-quality teaching and higher-quality student learning.

Will individual faculty members who have chosen to apply EBT be able to sustain these practices without fundamental changes in departmental, college, or institutional structures? We believe so. The concept and application of academic freedom ensures that individual faculty members

Table 1. Faculty Approaches to Teaching

Methods Used in "All" or "Most" Courses Taught	2005	2008	Percent Change
Cooperative learning (small groups)	47.8	59.1	11.3
Using real-life problems	n/a	55.7	n/a
Group projects	33.3	35.8	2.5
Multiple drafts of written work	24.8	24.9	0.1
Student evaluations of each other's work	16.0	23.5	7.5
Reflective writing/journaling	18.1	21.7	3.6
Electronic quizzes with immediate feedback in class	n/a	6.8	n/a
Extensive lecturing (not student centered)	55.2	46.4	−8.8

Source: Adapted from DeAngelo et al., 2009. p. 10.

have the authority to use instructional methods that they deem, based on their own professional judgments, effective in achieving their teaching and learning objectives. Use of teaching practices that are supported by evidence, although they may be nontraditional and uncommon, should be more justifiable to deans and department heads (and also to students who may have developed a degree of comfort with traditional teaching approaches) than practices based on tradition and common sense. To be sure, the primary purpose of this volume is to heighten faculty members' awareness of EBT in an effort to help them improve their teaching practices and thereby enhance their students' learning, thinking, and analytical skills as well as their motivation for, and enjoyment of, learning.

References

Ambrose, S. A., and others. *How Learning Works: Seven Research-Based Principles for Smart Teaching*. San Francisco: Jossey-Bass, 2010.

American Association of Colleges and Universities. *College Learning for the New Global Century: A Report from the National Leadership Council for Liberal Education and America's Promise*, 2007. http://www.hivcampuseducation.org/LEAP/documents/GlobalCentury_final.pdf

American Psychological Association. *Policy Statement on Evidence-Based Practice in Psychology*, 2005. http://www2.apa.org/practice/ebpstatement.pdf

Beder, H., and Medina, P. *Classroom Dynamics in Adult Literacy Education*. Cambridge, Mass.: National Center for the Study of Adult Learning and Literacy, 2001.

Biesta, G. "Why 'What Works' Won't Work: Evidence-Based Practice and the Democratic Deficit in Educational Research." *Educational Theory*, 2007, 57, 1–22.

Bok, D. C. *Our Underachieving Colleges: A Candid Look at How Much Students Learn and Why They Should Be Learning More*. Princeton, N.J.: Princeton University Press, 2006.

Boyer Commission on Educating Undergraduates in the Research University. *Reinventing undergraduate education: A blueprint for America's research universities.* Stony Brook: State University of New York. 1998. http://naples.cc.sunysb.edu/pres/boyer.nsf/

Bransford, J. D., Brown, A. L., and Cocking, R. R. (eds.). *How People Learn: Brain, Mind, Experience and School.* Washington, D.C.: National Academies Press, 2000.

Cole, R. *Manifesto for Evidence-Based Education.* Durham University Center for Evaluation and Monitoring, 1999. http://www.cemcentre.org/evidence-based -education/manifesto-for-evidence-based-education

DeAngelo, L., and others. *The American College Teacher: National Norms for the 2007–2008 HERI Faculty Survey.* Los Angeles: Higher Education Research Institute, 2009.

Friedman, T. *The World Is Flat 3.0: A Brief History of the Twenty-first Century.* New York: Picador, 2007.

Groccia, J. E. "Why Faculty Development? Why Now?" In A. Saroyan and M. Frenay (eds.), *Building Teaching Capacities in Universities: A Comprehensive International Model* (pp. 1–20). Sterling, Va.: Stylus, 2010.

Kazdin, A. E. "Evidence-Based Treatment and Practice: New Opportunities to Bridge Clinical Research and Practice, Enhance the Knowledge Base, and Improve Patient Care." *American Psychologist,* 2008, *63,* 146–159.

Kline, M. *Why the Professor Can't Teach: Mathematics and the Dilemma of University Education.* New York: St. Martin's Press, 1977.

LoBiondo-Wood, G., and Haber, J. *Nursing Research: Method and Critical Appraisal for Evidence-Based Practice.* (6th ed.) St. Louis, Mo.: Mosby, 2006.

Metz, A.J.R., Espiritu, R., and Moore, K. A. "What Is Evidence-Based Practice?" *Child Trends.* Washington, D.C.: Atlantic Philanthropies, 2007. www.childtrends.org

National Center for Public Policy on Higher Education (NCPPHE). *Measuring Up 2006: The National Report Card on Education,* 2006. http://measuringup.highereducation.org /_docs/2006/NationalReport_2006.pdf

National Center for Educational Statistics. *Digest of Educational Statistics 2007.* http:// nces.ed.gov/programs/digest/d07/ch_1.asp

Petty, G. *Evidence Based Teaching: A Practical Approach.* Bath, U.K.: Nelson Thornes, 2006.

Project on Student Debt. "Quick Facts about Student Debt." 2010. http://projectonstu dentdebt.org/files/File/Debt_Facts_and_Sources.pdf

Rischard, J. F. *High Noon: Twenty Global Issues, Twenty Years to Solve Them.* New York: Basic Books, 2002.

Sackett, D. L., and others. "Evidence Based Medicine: What It Is and What It Isn't." *British Medical Journal,* 1996, *321,* 71–72.

Slavin, R. E. "Perspectives on Evidence-Based Research in Education—What Works? Issues in Synthesizing Educational Program Evaluations." *Educational Researcher,* 2008, *37,* 5–14.

JAMES E. GROCCIA *is director of the Biggio Center for the Enhancement of Teaching and Learning and associate professor of Higher Education at Auburn University.*

WILLIAM BUSKIST *is the distinguished professor of the teaching of psychology and a faculty fellow at the Biggio Center for the Enhancement of Teaching and Learning at Auburn University.*

Academic lectures for the purpose of instruction maintain an important presence in most colleges and universities worldwide. This chapter examines the current state of the lecture and how learning sciences research can inform the most effective use of this method.

The Lecture

S. Raj Chaudhury

Most people tire of the lecture in ten minutes; clever people can do it in five. Sensible people never go to lectures at all.
                    —Canadian satirist Stephen Leacock

Leacock's quote (Sherin, 1995, p. 104) notwithstanding, several years ago I attended a memorable hour-long lecture. In his acceptance speech for an award from the American Association of Physics Teachers, physicist Dean Zollman recounted a lesson he learned from his daughter, Kim, when she visited his university (Zollman, 1996).

One day we were walking down a hallway, and Kim was looking in the rooms as a young, rather inquisitive girl does. She saw a scene which for her was very unusual—over a hundred students sitting in a room and watching one person talk. . . . She asked me the rather obvious question, "What are all those people doing?" I came up with what I thought was an excellent answer, "They're learning physics." Her response was "Do they just sit there?" (p. 114)

Zollman went on to share that

thinking about how people might learn physics was rather new to me, but I realized immediately that this question was profound. At the age of eight or nine she knew that just sitting there was not the way that people learned—it certainly wasn't the way that she learned. (p. 114)

NEW DIRECTIONS FOR TEACHING AND LEARNING, no. 128, Winter 2011 © Wiley Periodicals, Inc.
Published online in Wiley Online Library (wileyonlinelibrary.com) • DOI: 10.1002/tl.464

Zollman delivered his speech in a large hall attended by several hundred people, all of whom had substantial training in physics and experience in teaching it. No doubt that many of them, as I did, marveled at the power of this story and made mental notes to think further about this issue—how *do* our students learn when they sit in large lecture classes alongside scores of their classmates listening to one person talk? Zollman's lecture was inspiring, effective in delivering a message that I still remember, and at the time prompted further thought on an important issue in student learning.

Teachers rarely lecture under such optimal conditions. A typical fifteen-week semester might require instructors to deliver forty-five lectures to students who may have little background or interest in the subject matter. Other classes and distractions from work or co-curricular activities can further reduce the impact of learning from a lecture (Davis, 2009; Di Leonardi, 2007; Exley and Dennick, 2004; Svinicki and McKeachie, 2011).

In this chapter, I present evidence that the lecture can be an effective element of instructional practice. This chapter focuses on the lecture method, the delivery of information in an organized way to a large group of recipients by one person, and the lecture system, which includes the lecture along with specific activities involving students' active participation in learning the subject matter (McLeish, 1968).

Lecture Methods and Lecture Systems

The word "lecture" is derived from the Latin *lectare*, meaning "to read aloud." In medieval times, "a monk at a *lectern* would read out a book and the scholars would copy it down word for word" (Exley and Dennick, 2004, p. 3). It is astounding that the scene today in many college lecture halls is not all that much different. Broadwell (1980) provided a clue to the lecture method's longevity: "[I]t is virtually limitless in application, either to situation, subject matter or student age and learning ability" (p. xii).

Bligh (2000) conducted an extensive meta-review of the lecture literature in which he reviewed over one hundred studies comparing the lecture against other teaching methods (e.g., discussion, independent reading, inquiry projects). His main criterion for comparison was acquisition of information by students. The evidence supported Bligh's assertion that "the lecture is effective as any other method for transmitting information but not more effective" (p. 4).

Bligh's view of the role of students in lecture matched what Kim Zollman saw as she passed by the lecture hall: "[T]hey sit listening; their activity usually consists of selecting information from what is said, possibly translating it into their own words or some form of shorthand, and then writing it down" (Bligh, 2000, p. 9). However, because the lecture continues to be the primary method of instruction in introductory college courses, it is important that we look at ways in which modern lecture classrooms can become more effective environments for engaging students in learning.

Zollman's success in delivering a memorable lecture can possibly be explained by the fact that he presented relevant content for a motivated audience in an appropriate setting. In his talk, Zollman (1990) described how his daughter's comment led him to adapt the learning cycle (Karplus, 1980) based on Piagetian principles, to restructure a large-enrollment science course. The learning cycle is a pedagogical approach that promotes active inquiry and critical thinking. Each topical area is structured to have an exploration, a concept introduction, and an application phase. Zollman conducted the exploration and application phases outside of class in an activity center. Weekly lectures and assessments tied together the phases of the learning cycle.

Zollman (1990) compared student learning in two sections of the class: one taught by conventional lecture and one by the learning cycle method. He analyzed the final examination results by dividing the exam scores into four partial scores representing the major topics and by analyzing the exam in terms of the type of cognitive skills needed to answer the various questions. For all topic categories, the learning cycle group scored higher than the traditional lecture group. When analyzed for type of cognitive skills needed, the learning cycle group scored higher on conceptual explanations and calculations but lower on recall questions. This course model has continued to support strong conceptual learning in students even when multiple instructors have taught it over a period of twenty years. (D. A. Zollman, personal communication, October 5, 2010).

Applying Learning Sciences Research

Research from the learning sciences directly supports Zollman's learning cycle approach to the lecture system. In a National Research Council (NRC) review of evidence from scientific literatures on cognition, learning, development, culture, and the brain regarding human learning, Bransford, Brown, and Cocking (2000) recommended that teachers design their courses to be learner centered, knowledge centered, assessment centered, and community centered. By making meaningful connections between the content of lecture and student activities outside the classroom, Zollman built a robust lecture system.

According to Bransford and others (2000), a learner-centered environment design is consistent with evidence showing that learners use their current knowledge and beliefs to interpret new information. A knowledge-centered approach to instruction emphasizes that teachers should focus on developing students' abilities to think and solve problems with knowledge that is accessible and applied appropriately. Research also indicates that

NEW DIRECTIONS FOR TEACHING AND LEARNING • DOI: 10.1002/tl

feedback is fundamental to learning but is often absent in classrooms (e.g., Pellegrino, Chudowski, and Glaser, 2001). In an assessment-centered environment, students should be able to revise and improve the quality of their thinking and understanding. Finally, the NRC report urged that learning environments should foster a sense of community norms where students, teachers, and other participants value learning and high standards (see also Halpern and Hakel, 2003).

Some Interesting Variations on the Traditional Lecture

Although the NRC recommendations are applicable across disciplines, their implementation in the sciences has given rise to some interesting course designs that represent both small and large variations on the lecture method. For example, Mazur (1997) described his implementation of peer instruction (PI), an interactive student engagement strategy that utilizes a structured questioning process in enhancing student learning. Carefully chosen questions presented during lecture give students the opportunity to discover and correct their misunderstandings of the material and, in the process, learn the key ideas of physics from one another. Fagen, Crouch, and Mazur (2002) reported increased student mastery of both conceptual reasoning and quantitative problem solving using PI in teaching physics. Gains in student understanding were greatest when they used PI in combination with other strategies, such as reading incentives that connected lecture content to students' online responses to preassigned readings. The authors also reported nationwide learning gains from courses taught by other instructors who implemented PI.

Using a different approach, Udovic and others (2002) described a redesigned introductory biology course based on the "workshop" approach pioneered by Laws (1991) and Wilson (1994). In this course, the authors replaced almost all lecturing with student group problem solving and other projects. The traditionally taught control course met weekly for three regular fifty-minute lectures and one ninety-minute laboratory session. Over two years with the same instructor, the evidence showed that the inquiry-learning activities in the workshop course were more effective than the traditional course at helping students construct a robust understanding of fundamental concepts and an improved ability to use concepts to solve unfamiliar problems.

Likewise, Beichner and others (2007), the developers of Student-Centered Activities for Large Enrollment Undergraduate Programs (SCALE-UP), demonstrated significant learning gains on standard conceptual inventories of student learning in physics that compared favorably against national samples (Hake, 1998). The original implementation of this model placed ninety-nine students at eleven round tables working in groups of three on cognitively engaging tasks. The room design facilitated learner-centered teaching, and the curriculum materials facilitated knowledge-centered and assessment-centered teaching. Groups of students engaged in cognitively meaningful tasks formed a community of learners. Two aspects of this study are particularly noteworthy. First, students in the upper third of their class had the largest gains in learning, which demonstrated that an active learning approach was most beneficial for the highest achievers. Second, the failure rate for all students in the SCALE-UP class was one-third that of traditional lecture courses. Women and ethnic minorities were up to six times more likely to pass the reformed course than the traditional one. The SCALE-UP model has since been adopted for introductory science and engineering courses on many campuses with class sizes ranging from about fifty to over one hundred (Beichner and others, 2007).

In yet another study of interactive lecture systems, Knight and Wood (2005) performed a controlled study in an upper-division biology course in which approximately 30 to 40 percent of lecturing during class time was substituted with more engaging student-centered activities. Normalized learning gains (which allowed for comparison of students with different levels of incoming knowledge) calculated from pretest and posttest scores administered each semester indicated that the interactive approach was 33 percent superior to the traditional lecture method in boosting student achievement. Like Beichner and others (2007), Knight and Wood reported that students with grades of A or B had higher learning gains in the interactive course; C students achieved the same learning gain range in both types of courses.

Using clicker technology (Bruff, 2009; Duncan, 2005), Mayer and others (2009) examined whether the technique of "questioning" could be used successfully to foster generative learning in a large lecture general psychology class. The instructor asked two to four multiple-choice questions each class period that mirrored the type of questions students might see on the final exam. Mayer and coauthors investigated students' exam performance across three different sections of the course: a traditional lecture-based section with no in-class questions, a traditional lecture-based section using questions delivered and collected on paper, and a traditional lecture-based section where question responses were collected through clickers. There was no significant difference in the demographics or prior scholastic ability of the students across groups, and no other modifications were made to the course content. The same instructor taught the material for three consecutive years, which enabled the authors to examine whether students' cognitive skills could be assisted solely by a new technology.

The clicker treatment produced a gain of approximately one-third of a grade point over the other two conditions; the control conditions did not produce results that differed significantly from each other. This finding indicated that the questioning technique alone, when integrated into lecture (implemented on paper and somewhat disruptive to the class), was not so effective as the seamless integration of clicker-enabled questioning.

NEW DIRECTIONS FOR TEACHING AND LEARNING • DOI: 10.1002/tl

Student Attitudes Toward Lectures

Bligh (2000) found little compelling evidence that traditional lectures were effective in changing student attitudes toward the subject matter. Handelsman and others (2004) also pointed up that large lecture courses often do not contribute to fostering students' scientific curiosity, analytic thinking, and reasoning, key skills for future scientists. Redish, Saul, and Steinberg (1998) described results from the Maryland Physics Expectations Survey (MPEX), an instrument that probes student attitudes, beliefs, and assumptions about physics. Data from pre- and postinstruction surveys of 1,500 students enrolled at six universities indicated that scores often deteriorated by 5 to 10 percent after one semester of lecture-based introductory physics, whether the course had been modified to improve conceptual learning or not.

Redish and Hammer (2009) presented evidence of a promising approach that reversed this trend by focusing on lecture content, student engagement, and helping students learn how to learn science. They implemented three procedures that helped students modify their initial views on the nature of scientific knowledge and how to build physical intuition.

1. Explicit epistemological discussions tied a particular set of points presented by the instructor to a scientific process such as "sense making."
2. Modified PI (with clickers) included discussion with students about the kinds of thinking that could lead to their choosing incorrect responses to multiple-choice questions.
3. An adapted set of interactive lecture demonstration materials (Thornton and Sokoloff, 1998) emphasized the valid content of students' intuition and helped refine it.

In a follow-up study, Redish and Hammer (2009) evaluated student conceptual learning over multiple semesters and instructors and recorded normalized learning gains in the range shown by the stronger active engagement classes reported by Hake (1998). Student attitudes also shifted significantly toward experts' views of physics. These authors also reported that although there was initial resistance from students who had been successful in traditional courses, even the most vocal, accomplished students demonstrated understanding of the value of the instructors' epistemological approach at the conclusion of the semester.

Conclusions

Although the lecture method likely will continue to be a common method of teaching in higher education, the nature of the lecture is evolving from static formats in which students sit passively listening to the teacher speak

NEW DIRECTIONS FOR TEACHING AND LEARNING • DOI: 10.1002/tl

nonstop for fifty minutes to more dynamic and interactive sessions that require active student involvement in learning the subject matter. Miller, Pfund, Pribbenow, and Handelsman (2008) described an exciting interactive lecture technique for teaching biology in which the majority of class time is devoted to active learning activities delivered in units created by graduate students and postdoctoral fellows. Relative to students in control classes, students taught using this method showed gains in knowledge of specific subject areas, enhanced success in solving complex problems, and long-term retention of knowledge they learned months earlier. Thus, although there is no doubt that the lecture method remains an efficient way to deliver large amounts of information to large numbers of students, it is now apparent, based on empirical research on human learning, that lecture systems are currently evolving that enhance student engagement in the learning process and improve performance in most areas of student assessment.

Few teachers are able to deliver memorable, indeed inspirational, lectures like Zollman. The good news, however, is that all teachers can develop effective lecture-based systems, grounded in evidence-based practices, that stimulate and reinforce student learning and understanding in both the short and long term.

References

Beichner, R., and others. "The Student-Centered Activities for Large Enrollment Undergraduate Programs (SCALE-UP) Project." In E. Redish and P. Cooney (eds.), *Research-Based Reform of University Physics.* College Park, Md.: American Association of Physics Teachers, 2007, 1–42. http://www.per-central.org/document/ServeFile.cfm?ID=4517

Bligh, D. A. *What's the Use of Lectures?* San Francisco: Jossey-Bass, 2000.

Bransford, J., Brown, A. L., and Cocking, R. R. (eds.). *How People Learn: Brain, Mind, Experience, and School.* Washington, D.C.: National Academies Press, 2000.

Broadwell, M. M. *The Lecture Method of Instruction.* Englewood Cliffs, N.J.: Educational Technology, 1980.

Bruff, D. *Teaching with Classroom Response Systems.* San Francisco: Jossey-Bass, 2009.

Davis, B. G. *Tools for Teaching.* (2nd ed.) San Francisco: Jossey-Bass, 2009.

Di Leonardi, B. "Tips for Facilitating Learning: The Lecture Deserves Some Respect." *Journal of Continuing Education in Nursing,* 2007, 38, 154–161.

Duncan, D. *Clickers in the Classroom.* Boston: Addison-Wesley, 2005.

Exley, K., and Dennick, R. *Giving a Lecture: From Presenting to Teaching.* New York: Routledge Falmer, 2004.

Fagen, A. P., Crouch, C. H., and Mazur, E. "Peer Instruction: Results from a Range of Classrooms." *Physics Teacher,* 2002, 40, 206–209.

Hake, R. "Interactive-Engagement vs. Traditional Methods: A Six-Thousand-Student Survey of Mechanics Test Data for Introductory Physics Courses." *American Journal of Physics,* 1998, 66, 64–74.

Halpern, D., and Hakel, M. "Applying the Science of Learning to the University and Beyond." *Change,* July-Aug, 2003, 37–41.

Handelsman, J., and others. "Scientific Teaching." *Science,* 2004, 304, 521–522.

Karplus, R. "Teaching for the Development of Reasoning." *Research in Science Education,* 1980, 10(1), 1–9.

Knight, J. K., and Wood, W. B. "Teaching More by Lecturing Less." *Cell Biology Education,* 2005, *4,* 298–310.

Laws, P. "Calculus-Based Physics without Lectures." *Physics Today,* 1991, *44*(12), 24–31.

Mayer, R. E., and others. "Clickers in the Classroom: Fostering Learning with Questioning Methods in Large Lecture Classes." *Contemporary Educational Psychology,* 2009, *34,* 51–57.

Mazur, E. *Peer Instruction: A User's Manual.* Upper Saddle River, N.J.: Prentice Hall, 1997.

McLeish, J. *The Lecture Method.* Cambridge, U.K.: Cambridge Institute of Education, 1968.

Miller, S., Pfund, C., Pribbenow, C. M., and Handelsman, J. "Scientific Teaching in Practice." *Science,* 2008, *322,* 1329–1330.

Pellegrino, J. W., Chudowski, N., and Glaser, R., (eds.). (2001). *Knowing What Students Know.* Washington, D.C.: National Academies Press.

Redish, E. F., and Hammer, D. "Reinventing College Physics for Biologists: Explicating an Epistemological Curriculum," *American Journal of Physics,* 2009, *77,* 629–642.

Redish, E. F., Saul, J. M., and Steinberg, R. N. "Student Expectations in Introductory Physics." *American Journal of Physics,* 1998, *66,* 212–224.

Sherin, N. *Oxford Dictionary of Humorous Quotations.* Oxford, U.K.: Oxford University Press, 1995.

Svinicki, M., and McKeachie, W. J. *McKeachie's Teaching Tips: Strategies, Research, and Theory for College and University Teachers.* Belmont, Calif.: Wadsworth, 2011.

Thornton, R., and Sokoloff, D. "Using Interactive Lecture Demonstrations to Create an Active Learning Environment." *Physics Teacher,* 1998, *35,* 340–347.

Udovic, D., and others. "Workshop Biology: Demonstrating the Effectiveness of Active Learning in a Non-Majors Biology Course." *BioScience,* 2002, *52,* 272–281.

Wilson, J. M. "The CUPLE Physics Studio." *Physics Teacher,* 1994, *32,* 518–523.

Zollman, D. A. "Learning Cycles in a Large Enrollment Class." *Physics Teacher,* 1990, *28,* 20–25.

Zollman, D. A. "Do They Just Sit There? Reflections on Helping Students Learn Physics." *American Journal of Physics,* 1996, *64,* 114–119.

S. RAJ CHAUDHURY is associate director of the Biggio Center for the Enhancement of Teaching and Learning at Auburn University.

3

In problem-based learning, students working in collaborative groups learn by resolving complex, realistic problems under the guidance of faculty. In this chapter, we examine the evidence for effectiveness of the method to achieve its goals of fostering deep understandings of content and discuss the potential for developing process skills: research, negotiation and teamwork, writing, and verbal communication.

Problem-Based Learning

Deborah E. Allen, Richard S. Donham, Stephen A. Bernhardt

Problem-based learning (PBL) has wide currency on many college and university campuses, including our own, the University of Delaware. Although we would like to be able to claim clear evidence for PBL in terms of student learning outcomes, based on our review of the literature, we cannot state that research strongly favors a PBL approach, at least not if the primary evidence is subject matter learning.

There is some evidence of PBL effectiveness in medical school settings where it began, and there are numerous accounts of PBL implementation in various undergraduate contexts, replete with persuasively positive data from course evaluations (Duch, Groh, and Allen, 2001). However, evidence for learning outcomes is still needed. In this chapter, we review the origins of PBL, outline its characteristic methods, and suggest why we believe PBL has a persistent and growing influence among educators.

Origins of PBL in Medical Schools

PBL was formalized by medical educators in the 1950s and 1960s to address the exponential expansion of medical knowledge while better aligning traditional classroom problem-solving approaches with those used in clinical practice (Barrows and Tamblyn, 1980; Boud, 1985). Traditional approaches were based on the bucket theory (Wood, 1994): If medical students were filled with the requisite foundational knowledge, they would be able to strategically retrieve and direct just the right subsets of it toward problems of clinical practice. PBL was designed to address the underlying flaws of the bucket theory, especially leaky, overflowing, or inappropriately

NEW DIRECTIONS FOR TEACHING AND LEARNING, no. 128, Winter 2011 © Wiley Periodicals, Inc.
Published online in Wiley Online Library (wileyonlinelibrary.com) • DOI: 10.1002/tl.465

filled buckets. By presenting complex case histories typical of real patients as the pretext for learning, PBL demanded that students call on an integrated, multidisciplinary knowledge base (Wood, 1994).

In the idealized learning cycle of medical school PBL (Engle, 1999), students working in teams learn by solving real or realistic problems. Students grapple with a multistage, complex medical case history, which offers an engaging and memorable context for learning. As they define the problem's scope and boundaries, student teams identify and organize relevant ideas and prior knowledge. The teams form questions based on self-identified gaps in their knowledge, and they use these questions to guide subsequent independent research outside the classroom, with research tasks parceled out among team members. When the students reconvene, they present and discuss their findings, integrating their new knowledge and skills into the problem context. As they move through the stages of a complex problem, they continue to define new areas of needed learning in pursuit of a solution. In the case of this original PBL model, a solution is an accurate diagnosis and recommendation of successful treatment of the patient.

PBL continues to be a favored method in many medical schools. What became evident in effectiveness studies was that there was no simple answer to the question "Is PBL better than traditional methods?" Several meta-analyses of the data suggested that PBL has modest or no beneficial effect on student learning of content (from the United States Medical Licensing Examination [USMLE] Step 1—basic science understanding; Albanese and Mitchell, 1993; Nandi and others, 2000; Vernon and Blake, 1993). In fact, it appears that students in a traditional medical program sometimes, but not consistently, slightly outperform their PBL counterparts.

However, disaggregation of the data suggests an underlying richness that is not captured simply by looking at student achievement on content recall exams. If, for example, scores on the USMLE Step 2 (knowledge of clinical practice) or ability to apply knowledge in the clinic after graduation are considered, medical school students with PBL experience frequently outperform their traditional counterparts (Albanese and Mitchell, 1993; Dochy, Segers, Van den Bossche, and Gijbels, 2003; Koh, Khoo, Wong, and Koh, 2008; Vernon and Blake, 1993). Recent meta-analyses have begun to tease apart some of the relative merits of PBL and suggest that the most positive effects are seen with student understanding of the organizing principles that link concepts in the knowledge domain being studied (Gijbels, Dochy, Van den Bossche, and Segers, 2005). Dochy and others (2003) reported a robust positive effect from PBL on the skills of students, noting that, intriguingly, students in PBL remember more acquired knowledge compared with their traditional counterparts. The early meta-analyses of PBL outcomes in the medical school setting (Albanese and Mitchell, 1993; Vernon and Blake, 1993) also document positive student attitudes about learning, with students frequently viewing PBL as both a challenging and a motivating approach.

Strategies for PBL Implementation

Because PBL explicitly addresses some of the shortcomings of science education, it migrated into undergraduate science and engineering classrooms (Woods, 1985). It then expanded into basic as well as applied fields as well as into the humanities and social sciences (Duch and others, 2001). With the introduction of PBL to undergraduate courses, teachers modified the method to accommodate larger class sizes, greater student diversity, timing and scheduling issues, multiple classroom groups, and lack of suitable classroom space (Allen, Duch, and Groh, 1996).

PBL requires a shift in the educational paradigm for faculty. In PBL, the role of the instructor shifts from presenter of information to facilitator of a problem-solving process. Although the PBL process calls on students to become self-directed learners, faculty facilitators guide them by monitoring discussion and intervening when appropriate, asking questions that probe accuracy, relevance, and depth of information and analyses; raising new (or neglected) issues for consideration; and fostering full and even participation (Mayo, Donnelly, and Schwartz, 1995).

Instead of lecturing, PBL instructors must find or create good problems based on clear learning goals. Through these problems, instructors lead students to learn key concepts, facts, and processes related to core course content. PBL problems must be carefully constructed—not only to present students with issues and dilemmas that matter to them but also to foster their development of conceptual frameworks (Hung, Jonassen, and Liu, 2007). PBL problems may intentionally pose cognitive challenges by not providing all the information needed, thereby motivating a self-directed search for explanations. Instructors often allow students considerable latitude to make false starts and wrong turns. Well-developed, peer-reviewed problems can be found at the PBL Clearinghouse (University of Delaware, 2010).

Successful implementation of PBL is critically dependent on the instructor's scaffolding of students' active learning and knowledge construction (Amador, Miles, and Peters, 2006; Duch and others, 2001). For example, PBL instructors can plan for intervals of class discussion or mini-lectures to help students navigate conceptual impasses, to dig more deeply into certain topics, or to find useful resources. Instructors can enter team discussions to listen and pose questions (Hmelo-Silver, Duncan, and Chinn, 2007). They can also use student facilitators to extend their instructional reach.

Importantly, PBL can support the development of a range of "soft" skills: research skills, negotiation and teamwork, reading, writing, and oral communication. Cooperative learning strategies that foster effective

NEW DIRECTIONS FOR TEACHING AND LEARNING • DOI: 10.1002/tl

teamwork become critical, as does the need for everyone to work to keep team members engaged and on track (Johnson, Johnson, and Smith, 1998). PBL classrooms are particularly well suited to the development of writing abilities. PBL instructors tend to rely on authentic assessment, with most problems leading up to a demonstration or presentation of learning, often taking the form of a written product: a solution, a recommendation, a summary of what was learned, or some other form of group or individual reporting. To encourage development of writing skills, thinking skills, and learning in general, instructors can call for students to produce specific genres of writing: progress reports, schedules, task lists, meeting minutes, abstracts, literature reviews, proofs, lab reports, data analyses, and technical briefings (Klein, 1999). Alaimo, Bean, Langenhan, and Nichols (2009) showed how to integrate writing as a core activity in an inquiry-based chemistry course, demonstrating strong learning outcomes in the process.

Instructors must also encourage good team communication strategies. Teams must avoid reaching premature closure or succumbing to group-think—where a group seizes on a path because a team member is forceful or persuasive. The teams that perform best are those that generate and sustain consideration of multiple alternatives, engaging in and sustaining "substantive conflict" (Burnett, 1991).

Effectiveness of PBL on Content Learning in Undergraduate Settings

Confusion and lack of specification about what PBL is as it is actually practiced in the classroom hampers analysis of the effect of PBL on the acquisition of content learning. In particular, PBL adopters in undergraduate settings, grappling with the difficulties of monitoring multiple classroom groups, hybridize the method in various ways to incorporate aspects of discussion and case study method teaching (Silverman and Welty, 1990). Instructors tend to insert highly choreographed segments of instructor-centered, whole-class discussions into the PBL cycle and to interpose PBL problems intermittently throughout the course schedule, blended with more traditional instruction (Duch and others, 2001). As Newman (2003) noted, this hybridization of PBL makes it "difficult to distinguish between different types of PBL and even to distinguish between PBL and other educational interventions" (p. 7).

Nevertheless, there are scattered reports of positive outcomes. In a study of over 6,500 students, Hake (1998) found that interactive engagement methods (broadly defined as heads-on, hands-on activities with immediate feedback) were strongly superior to lecture-centered instruction in improving performance on valid and reliable mechanics tests used to assess students' understanding of physics. Williams (2001) reported gains in the Force Concept Inventory for students in a PBL course that are consistent with the averages in other introductory physics courses that use interactive engagement methods. Palaez (2002) observed that students in a PBL biology course with an intensive writing component outperformed students in a course using traditional lecture-based instruction on exams that assessed conceptual understandings.

Although there is less research on undergraduate learning than in medical education, the data support the broad conclusion that PBL may show only modest benefits on recalled content knowledge, but it positively influences integration of new knowledge with existing knowledge. However, faculty members frequently adopt PBL to help students develop life-long learning skills. These skills are exercised routinely in the natural course of the PBL learning cycle. Given these additional but divergent student learning goals, many faculty members are satisfied with student content learning that is similar or not significantly decreased when using PBL. At the very least, these findings assuage any residual concerns they or others may have that spending time on these ambitious process objectives undermines the learning of essential course content.

Effectiveness of PBL on Process Skills

Because PBL engages students in a range of soft skills, perhaps other positive learning outcomes can be claimed for the method. A case in point is the benefit of using cooperative learning groups on such general aspects of academic success as retention as well as on fostering positive student attitudes about learning (Springer, Stanne, and Donovan, 1999). Another is the use of writing-to-learn strategies in PBL. Incorporation of short, in-class writing assignments improves student performance on traditional concept and content-based exams (Butler, Phillmann, and Smart, 2001; Davidson and Pearce, 1990; Drabick, Weisberg, Paul, and Bubier, 2007; Stewart, Myers, and Culley, 2010).

There is some evidence that systemic and sustained use of PBL in the classroom fosters cognitive growth. Downing and others (2009) followed two parallel cohorts of students in degree programs, one taught with PBL, the other by traditional methods, and found greater gains in metacognitive skills in the PBL group. Tiwari, Lai, So, and Yurn (2006) similarly reported significant differences in the development of undergraduate nursing students' critical thinking dispositions in a PBL versus a lecture-based course, as determined by comparisons of pre- and posttest scores on the California Critical Thinking Disposition Inventory.

Effectiveness of PBL on Student Engagement

Widespread agreement is emerging that at the core of effective teaching are activities that engage students by challenging them academically and involving them intensely, within supportive environments that provide multiple opportunities for interactions with faculty, peers, and members of

NEW DIRECTIONS FOR TEACHING AND LEARNING • DOI: 10.1002/tl

the surrounding community (Smith, Sheppard, Johnson, and Johnson, 2005). Because PBL uses an assortment of methods associated with student engagement—active, collaborative, student-centered, and self-directed learning focused on realistic problems and authentic assessments—we might expect that it would lead to increased student engagement. By requiring students to talk to each other and collaborate on projects important to their academic success, PBL addresses student alienation and failure to form social networks, major reasons for students dropping out of college (Tinto, 1994). Two systematic analyses of students' perceptions of the immediate and longer-term value and transferability of the reasoning and processing skills they developed during PBL courses (using the National Study of Student Engagement survey [NSSE] or a similarly designed instrument) in fact provide support for characterization of PBL as a pedagogy of engagement (Ahlfeldt, Mehta, and Sellnow, 2005; Murray and Summerlee, 2007).

An important aspect of engagement is students' ability to practice self-regulated or lifelong learning behaviors (Smith et al., 2005): the ability to define what to learn and to effectively use the time and resource management needed to learn it. Blumberg's (2000) review of the literature described numerous instances of documented gains in these areas that can be attributed to students' PBL experiences.

Incorporating writing tasks into PBL problems also shows promise for enhancing student engagement. Butler and others (2001) found that short, in-class microthemes increased positive motivation to attend class and increased student engagement. Additionally, Light (2001) found that writing increases the time students spend on a course, increases the extent to which they are intellectually challenged, and increases their level of interest. Confirming Light's findings are the very compelling data emerging from the NSSE (Gonyea, Anderson, Anson, and Paine, 2010). NSSE personnel worked with writing faculty to develop a special set of add-on questions concerning writing to the spring 2009 administration of NSSE. The data strongly supported writing as the single most important determinant of engaged, deep learning. When the independent variable is assigning meaning-constructing writing tasks, the NSSE data show moderate to strong effects on increased higher-order thinking, integrative learning, and reflective learning.

Conclusions

There is broad support for the conclusion that PBL methods enhance the affective domain of student learning, improve student performance on complex tasks, and foster better retention of knowledge. We would argue that more research is needed, research that is sensitive to the range of outcomes that we have discussed. For example, we would like to see additional research into the effects of PBL on student performance on state board examinations and on students' gains in problem-solving, critical thinking, motivation, and self-regulated learning. Another important area of future research would identify the particular PBL implementation methods that lead to improved outcomes.

PBL continues to enjoy popularity among a wide range of instructors across numerous disciplines at many institutions. Because PBL changes the nature of teaching and learning, many instructors embrace the method without clear, confirming evidence of its effectiveness. In essence, they like being freed to work within a different classroom model, one where students are active and in control of learning. They like their role as consultant or facilitator better than their previous role of lecturer. The PBL classroom is, after all, a place that is lively with controversy, debate, and peer-to-peer communication—providing both faculty and students with immediate and unmistakable evidence of their competencies and understandings of and about what matters.

References

Ahlfeldt, S., Mehta, S., and Sellnow, T. "Measurement and Analysis of Student Engagement in University Classes where Varying Levels of PBL Methods of Instruction Are in Use." *Higher Education Research and Development,* 2005, *24,* 5–20.

Alaimo, P. J., Bean, J. C., Langenhan, J. M., and Nichols, L. "Eliminating Lab Reports: A Rhetorical Approach for Teaching the Scientific Paper in Sophomore Organic Chemistry." *WAC Journal,* 2009, *20,* 17–32.

Albanese, M. S., and Mitchell, S. "Problem-Based Learning: A Review of Literature on Its Outcomes and Implementation Issues." *Academic Medicine,* 1993, *68,* 52–81.

Allen, D. E., Duch, B. J., and Groh, S. E. "The Power of Problem-Based Learning in Teaching Introductory Science Courses." In L. Wilkerson and W. H. Gijselaers (eds.), *Bringing Problem-Based Learning to Higher Education: Theory and Practice.* New Directions for Teaching and Learning Series, no. 68. San Francisco: Jossey-Bass, 1996.

Amador, J. A., Miles, L., and Peters, C. B. *The Practice of Problem-Based Learning: A Guide to Implementing PBL in the College Classroom.* Bolton, Mass.: Anker, 2006.

Barrows, H., and Tamblyn, R. *Problem-based Learning: An Approach to Medical Education.* New York: Springer, 1980.

Blumberg, P. "Evaluating the Evidence that Problem-Based Learners Are Self-Directed Learners: Review of the Literature." In D. H. Evensen and C. E. Hmelo (eds.), *Problem-Based Learning: A Research Perspective on Learning Interactions* (pp. 199–222). Mahwah, N.J.: Lawrence Erlbaum, 2000.

Boud, D. J. "Problem-Based Learning in Perspective. In D. Boud (ed.), *Problem-Based Learning in Education for the Professions* (pp. 13–18). Sydney, Australia: HERDSA, 1985.

Burnett, R. E. "Substantive Conflict in a Cooperative Context: A Way to Improve the Collaborative Planning of Workplace Documents." *Technical Communication,* 1991, *38,* 532–539.

Butler, A., Phillmann, K.-B., and Smart, L. "Active Learning within a Lecture: Assessing the Impact of Short, In-Class Writing Exercises." *Teaching of Psychology,* 2001, *28,* 57–59.

Davidson, D., and Pearce, D. "Perspectives on Writing Activities in the Mathematics Classroom." *Mathematics Education Research Journal,* 1990, *2,* 15–22.

Dochy, F., Segers, M., Van den Bossche, P., and Gijbels, D. "Effects of Problem-Based Learning: A Meta-Analysis." *Learning and Instruction,* 2003, *13,* 533–568.

Downing, K., and others. "Problem-Based Learning and the Development of Metacognition." *Higher Education,* 2009, *57,* 609–621,

Drabick, D.A.G., Weisberg, R., Paul, L., and Bubier, J. L. "Keeping It Short and Sweet: Brief, Ungraded Writing Assignments Facilitate Learning." *Teaching of Psychology,* 2007, *34,* 172–176.

Duch, B., Groh, S. E., and Allen, D. E. (eds.). *The Power of Problem-Based Learning: A Practical "How-to" for Teaching Undergraduate Courses in Any Discipline.* Sterling, Va.: Stylus, 2001.

Engle, C. E. "Not Just a Method but a Way of Learning." In D. Boud and G. Feletti (eds.), *The Challenge of Problem-Based Learning* (pp. 17–27). London: Kogan Page, 1999.

Gijbels, D., Dochy, F., Van den Bossche, P., and Segers, M. "Effects of Problem-Based Learning: A Meta-Analysis from the Angle of Assessment." *Review of Educational Research,* 2005, *75,* 27–61.

Gonyea, R., Anderson, P., Anson, C., and Paine, C. "Powering Up Your WAC Program: Practical, Productive Ways to Use Assessment Data from NSSE's Consortium for the Study of Writing in College." Paper presented at the 10th International Writing across the Curriculum Conference, Bloomington, Indiana, May 2010.

Hake, R. "Interactive Engagement versus Traditional Methods: A Six Thousand-Student Survey of Mechanics Test Data for Introductory Physics Courses." *American Journal of Physics,* 1998, *66,* 64–74.

Hmelo-Silver, C. E., Duncan, R. G., and Chinn, C. A. "Scaffolding and Achievement in Problem-based and Inquiry Learning: A Response to Kirschner, Sweller, and Clark (2006)." *Educational Psychologist,* 2007, *42,* 99–107.

Hung, W., Jonassen, D. H., and Liu, R. "Problem-based Learning." In J. M. Spector, J. van Merrienboer, M. D. Merrill, and M. P. Driscoll (eds.), *Handbook of Research for Educational Communications and Technology* (pp. 485–505). Mahwah, N.J.: Lawrence Erlbaum, 2007.

Johnson, D. W., Johnson, R. T., and Smith, K. A. "Cooperative Learning Returns to College: What Evidence Is There that It Works?" *Change,* July-Aug. 1998, 27–35.

Klein, P. D. "Reopening Inquiry into Cognitive Processes in Writing-to-Learn." *Educational Psychology Review,* 1999, *11,* 203–270.

Koh, G.C.-H., Khoo, H. E., Wong, M. L., and Koh, D. "The Effects of Problem-Based Learning During Medical School on Physician Competency: A Systematic Review." *Canadian Medical Association Journal,* 2008, *178,* 34–41.

Light, R. J. *Making the Most of College.* Cambridge, Mass.: Harvard University Press, 2001.

Mayo, W. P., Donnelly, M. B., and Schwartz, R. W. "Characteristics of the Ideal Problem-Based Learning Tutor in Clinical Medicine." *Evaluation and the Health Professions,* 1995, *18,* 124–136.

Murray, J., and Summerlee, A. "The Impact of Problem-based Learning in an Interdisciplinary First-Year Program on Student Learning Behaviour." *Canadian Journal of Higher Education,* 2007, *37,* 87–107.

Nandi, P. L., and others. "Undergraduate Medical Education: Comparison of Problem-Based Learning and Conventional Teaching." *Hong Kong Medical Journal,* 2000, *6,* 301–306.

Newman, M. "A Pilot Systematic Review and Meta-Analysis on the Effectiveness of Problem Based Learning." *On Behalf of Campbell Collaboration Systemic Review Group on the Effectiveness of Problem-based Learning.* Newcastle upon Tyne, U.K.: University of Newcastle upon Tyne, 2003. http://www.ltsn-01.ac.uk/static/uploads/resources /pbl_report.pdf

Pelaez, N. J. "Problem-Based Writing with Peer Review Improves Academic Performance in Physiology." *Advances in Physiology Education*, 2002, *26*(3), 174–184.

Silverman, R., and Welty, W. H. "Teaching with Cases." *Journal on Excellence in College Teaching*, 1990, *1*, 88–97.

Smith, K. A., Sheppard, S. D., Johnson, D. W., and Johnson, R. T. "Pedagogies of Engagement: Classroom-Based Practices." *Journal of Engineering Education*, 2005, *94*, 1–15.

Springer, L., Stanne, M. E., and Donovan, S. S. "Measuring the Success of Small-Group Learning on Undergraduates in Science, Mathematics, Engineering and Technology: A Meta-Analysis." *Review of Educational Research*, 1999, *69*, 21–51.

Stewart, T. L., Myers, A. C., and Culley, M. R. "Enhanced Learning and Retention Through 'Writing to Learn' in the Psychology Classroom." *Teaching of Psychology*, 2010, *37*, 46–49.

Tinto, V. *Leaving College: Rethinking the Causes and Cures of Student Attrition* (2nd ed.). Chicago: University of Chicago Press, 1994.

Tiwari, A., Lai, P., So, M., and Yurn, K. "A Comparison of the Effects of Problem-based Learning and Lecturing on the Development of Students' Critical Thinking." *Medical Education*, 2006, *40*, 547–554.

University of Delaware. *PBL Clearinghouse*, 2010. https://primus.nss.udel.edu/Pbl/

Vernon, D.T.A., and Blake, R. L. "Does Problem-Based Learning Work? A Meta-Analysis of Evaluative Research." *Academic Medicine*, 1993, *68*, 550–563.

Williams, B. A. "Introductory Physics: A Problem-Based Model." In B. J. Duch, S. E. Groh, and D. E. Allen (eds.), *The Power of Problem-Based Learning* (pp. 251–269). Sterling, Va.: Stylus, 2001.

Wood, E. J. "The Problems of Problem-Based Learning." *Biochemical Education*, 1994, *22*, 78–82.

Woods, D. "Problem-Based Learning and Problem-Solving. In D. Boud (ed.), *Problem-Based Learning for the Professions* (pp. 19–42). Sydney, Australia: Higher Education Research and and Development Society of Australasia, 1985.

DEBORAH E. ALLEN *is an associate professor of biological sciences at the University of Delaware.*

RICHARD S. DONHAM *is senior science education associate at the Mathematics and Science Education Resource Center at the University of Delaware.*

STEPHEN A. BERNHARDT *is the Andrew B. Kirkpatrick Jr. chair in writing and professor of English at the University of Delaware.*

NEW DIRECTIONS FOR TEACHING AND LEARNING • DOI: 10.1002/tl

This chapter describes the history of case study teaching, types of cases, and experimental data supporting their effectiveness. It also describes a model for comparing the efficacy of the various case study methods.

Case Study Teaching

Clyde Freeman Herreid

One hundred years ago, Harvard Business School initiated a novel approach to teaching called the case study method. Patterned after the use of cases in its law school, the business faculty started using true stories of business practices to instruct students. In the classroom, students analyzed the details of a business problem with the professor in a Socratic dialogue. This methodology became known as the case method and is commonly practiced in that form today in graduate schools of law, public policy, and business.

The case study method has morphed significantly since that time. In the hands of Harvard professor of chemistry James Conant in the 1940s, instruction by the exclusive use of stories was delivered via didactic lecture. In the newly created Medical College of McMaster University in Canada in the late 1960s, the exclusive use of stories became known as problem-based learning (PBL): Students met in small groups with a facilitator and together diagnosed their patients' ailments. These formalized teaching methods used stories to present their teaching message. Recognizing this common thread, we classify all of these approaches and others as variants of the initial Harvard model of student engagement by teaching in context. Simply stated, "Case studies are stories with an educational message" (Herreid, 2007, p. xiv).

This material is based on work supported by the NSF under Grant No. DUE-0618570. Any opinions, findings, conclusions, or recommendations expressed in this material are those of the author and do not necessarily reflect the views of the National Science Foundation.

When cases are defined in this way, it is apparent that the stories can be told in a variety of ways: by discussion, lecture, small-group methods, and a host of others, including the use of clickers in large classes. The common element is the use of stories. This approach frees instructors to be creative, unfettered by rules of presentation. It also has led to difficulties in evaluation because so many diverse methods are often lumped together as case studies.

Case Study Methods

A brief taxonomy of case study methods based on the way the instructor presents the story in the classroom (Herreid, 1994, 1998, 2005b) follows.

Lecture Method. In the lecture method, the instructor takes on the role of storyteller. An advantage of the method is that the information is presented in context. It is Professor Conant regaling his students with accounts of the great historical discoveries in science. In its most dramatic incarnation, it is biology professor Richard Eatkin of Berkeley in the 1970s impersonating historical figures in class. Albeit more engaging than the usual instructor-speak, it still has the disadvantages of the lecture method: Students are passive recipients of information.

Discussion Methods. Whole classroom discussion is the classical case teaching method. In its original form, it was conducted by a professor in the front of the class who called on anxious students to discuss the case at hand, hoping that brilliant thoughts would flower amid the weeds of discourse. It can be conducted as a cross-examination, as exemplified by Professor Kingsfield in the movie and television series *The Paper Chase* or conducted in more student-friendly forms. Other classroom variants of the entire classroom discussion format include debates, symposia, trials, and public hearing.

Small-Group Methods. Over the past two decades, the advantages of small-group discussion has been promoted as collaborative or cooperative learning and championed by the Johnson brothers in a series of books (e.g., Johnson, Johnson, and Smith, 2006). They have gathered extensive data showing that teaching using small groups of students beats the lecture method hands down (e.g., Johnson and Johnson, 1989). It is especially effective in promoting diversity of opinion and respect for divergent views and for improving the expression of ideas.

Training medical students using PBL is the best-known small-group case approach (e.g., Barrows and Tamblyn, 1980). In its original form, teams of students worked exclusively with tutors to diagnose patient ailments, typically receiving information over several class periods with opportunities to do literature research. A popular variation of this method of providing information piecemeal (often called progressive disclosure) is the interrupted case method (Herreid, 2005a). It is similar to PBL, but each case is handled in a single class without students' doing a literature search.

NEW DIRECTIONS FOR TEACHING AND LEARNING • DOI: 10.1002/tl

Instead, the case contains in its successive parts all of the information and data that students need to solve the problem in a stepwise fashion.

The intimate debate method (i.e., "constructive controversy") is a small-group approach that is effective in dealing with controversial topics, such as stem cell research, creation versus evolution, global warming, or the medicinal use of marijuana (Herreid and DuRei, 2007). Teams of students prepare both pro and con sides of an issue. They then pair off with another pair of students on the opposite side of the question and argue from their particular viewpoints. Then the student pairs reverse roles. Finally they abandon their advocacy roles and try to reach a compromise on the question.

Larry Michaelsen has elevated the use of small groups to an art form called team learning (Michaelsen, Knight, and Fink, 2002). Prior to each class, students have a reading assignment. When they enter the class, they assemble into their permanent small groups, take an individual quiz based on the reading material, then retake the quiz in their small groups. The quizzes are graded in class immediately, and the groups have a chance to appeal their grades in writing. Case studies enter the picture when students apply what they have learned in their previous preparatory reading.

Individual Cases. Not all cases need be given to groups. Here are three examples where most of the work is done by individuals. In the dialogue case method, the professor asks students to write a dialogue between two well-versed people on a controversial topic (Herreid, 2006). The individuals in their story (say Sally and Sam) hold opposite views on a question such as global warming. Sally and Sam have at least twenty exchanges, twenty from Sally and twenty from Sam. The exchanges should be substantive and intelligent. The students must reference any claims that their protagonists make. Finally, at the end of the dialogue, the students should declare their own position on the topic and their reasons for it.

In the direct case method, the case is given to the entire class, but students work on it alone (Cliff and Wright, 1996). The case itself is a brief scenario with a series of questions. Each question has a single, correct answer. In other words, the case is not open-ended with multiple possible answers where reasonable people may differ. Instead, the purpose of the case is to emphasize factual information. This type of case is especially appropriate for teachers of anatomy and physiology, where a premium is placed on the transfer of information. Such courses often include topic modules on circulation, respiration, digestion, and the like. At the beginning of each module, the instructor gives a brief case vignette with questions that students must answer. Students hand in their responses after hearing the lectures on the topic and doing literature research. The instructor then runs a class discussion on their responses.

Computer Simulation Cases. Bergland and others (2006) developed computer-based interactive cases (http://caseit.uwrf.edu//caseit.html) that may last as long as a month, with time for independent student research, communication, and writing. They designed "Case It!" to enhance learning about genetics and infectious disease; it is freely available at http://caseit .uwrf.edu/. There are three separate tools for students: With Case It! Investigator, students view video cases and gather background information. With Case-It! Simulation, students simulate laboratory tests of several genetic and infectious diseases. With Case It! Launch Pad, students access a Web page editor or Internet conferencing system. After running analyses using Case It! Simulation, students take photos of the resulting gels and blots and incorporate them into Web pages via the Web page editor. They construct Web page posters reporting results of this testing, explaining the results to the case "patients" and giving treatment and ethical/social advice. During Web conferencing, students play the role of laboratory technicians, counselors, or doctors when they respond to questions raised about their Web posters, then they switch roles to that of a family member or patient when asking questions about the Web posters created by their peers.

Clicker Cases. Introductory classes, the bread-and-butter courses for universities, are almost prohibitively large, often with several hundred souls crammed into a fixed-seat auditorium. Running a classroom discussion or forming small-group conversations requires heroic effort. The advent of audience response systems (aka "clickers") has been a salvation. Students, each holding a radio frequency clicker (similar to a television remote), can type in a response to a multiple-choice question that a professor asks on a PowerPoint slide. The classroom computer receives and tallies the responses and displays them on a screen in real time. The data may be anonymous or keyed to individual students. With the use of this technology, case studies can be presented to huge classes just as in the interrupted case method. Professors can ask students to respond to the questions as the case, presented in a PowerPoint presentation, unfolds. Clicker cases have opened up the megaclassrooms to truly interactive experiences (Herreid, 2006).

Review of the Empirical Evidence

Amazingly, the case method in law, business, and public policy has seldom been evaluated. In contrast, once scientists began to use cases in their variable guises, data on the method's effectiveness began to appear. PBL is the most studied of all of the case approaches; it is considered in detail in the article by Allen, Donham, and Bernhardt in this volume. Suffice it to say, because of the many ways that PBL is implemented, there is more variation in the data than one would wish. Meta-analyses invariably lump anything that is called PBL into the same category, regardless of the form of presentation. Nonetheless, there seems to be a general consensus that students in PBL classes do slightly less well on multiple-choice exams but better in open-ended questioning than students taught by lecture (Dochy, Segers, Van den Bossche, and Gijbels, 2003).

The same situation appears to be true for case-based teaching. Kim and others (2006) conducted a meta-analysis of 100 case articles and found enormous variation in teaching methodology. They concluded that there was little evidence that the use of cases improved critical-thinking skills. They did not find one article in the field of basic science, which is remarkable because important literature on this matter does, in fact, exist.

Lundeberg and Yadav (2006a, 2006b) summarized what we know about case teaching. We know the most about affective measures (that is, student and faculty attitudes about it). For example, Yadav and others (2007) reported data on a national survey of 101 faculty members from twenty-three states and Canada who used cases. Faculty members reported that case-based teaching led to students' stronger critical-thinking skills (89.1 percent), better ability to make connections across multiple content areas (82.6 percent), and deeper understanding of concepts (90.1 percent). Faculty members also reported that during case study teaching, students were better able to view an issue from multiple perspectives (91.3 percent) and were more engaged in the class when using cases (93.8 percent).

Clicker cases have received much recent attention. In a series of three papers, a coalition of authors from a dozen schools compared the results of eight clicker cases in a general biology course to the same material presented via traditional lectures (Kang and others, 2009; Lundeberg and others, 2009; Wolter and others, 2011). These authors collected data from over 1,000 students and found that:

1. Faculty can effectively use case studies in large classes of well over 100 students when clickers are used.
2. For most of the class topics that faculty taught using cases (for example, cell theory, cell division, Mendelian genetics, cancer), students showed greater learning than with lecture, but not all (for example, DNA; the reason for this finding is not clear but may depend on how compelling the story line of the case is).
3. Faulty perceptions of what makes a good case suggest that cases with emotional engagement promote the greatest learning.
4. Students rate very favorably the use of a combination of clickers and cases as a teaching approach.
5. Clicker cases appear to have a greater appeal and to produce greater learning in women and nonmajors than in men and majors.

These findings are consistent with previous studies in which investigators have studied separately the value of clickers or the use of active learning strategies (for example, Hake, 1998; Kay and LeSage, 2009; Patry, 2009).

On the basis of this research, we can make three generalizations:

1. Active learning techniques, as exemplified by case studies, are superior and often strikingly superior to the lecture method, which begs the

question, "Why are we still using lectures?" (See the article by Chaudhury in this volume.)

2. Case studies (including PBL) are among the best studied of all of the active learning approaches. Their greatest strength seems to be that they put learning into a context that is memorable.

3. There are many different case teaching methods. When researchers write review papers, they often lump all of them together under the case or PBL method. Thus, we have essentially no knowledge of their relative individual effectiveness. Still, however, we can make some guesses about effectiveness, using the Cone of Learning as a frame of reference.

Case Studies and the Cone of Learning

The left side of Figure 1 shows Dale's (1969) Cone of Learning model, a model that has some experimental support (Lord, 2007). It depicts how the various methods of teaching affect the retention of information. Note the striking ineffectiveness of the lecture method compared with other strategies. In contrast, the greatest retention occurs when students interact with one another. So in answer to the question "What is the most effective method of teaching?" Bill McKeachie had it right when he said that the best answer "is that it depends on the goal, the student, the content, and the

Figure 1. Cone of Learning

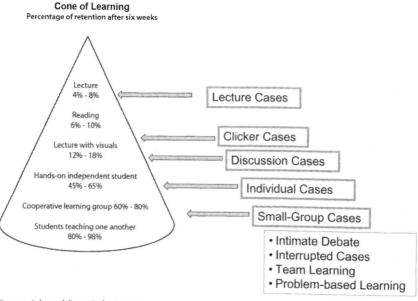

Cone of Learning
Percentage of retention after six weeks

Lecture
4% - 8%

Reading
6% - 10%

Lecture with visuals
12% - 18%

Hands-on independent student
45% - 65%

Cooperative learning group 60% - 80%

Students teaching one another
80% - 98%

Lecture Cases

Clicker Cases

Discussion Cases

Individual Cases

Small-Group Cases

• Intimate Debate
• Interrupted Cases
• Team Learning
• Problem-based Learning

Source: Adapted from Dale, 1969.

teacher. But the next best answer is, 'students teaching other students'" (Svinicki and McKeachie, 2011, p. 192)

Now here is the question: If we grant that the Cone of Learning illustrates the real state of affairs with regard to student learning, then where do the various styles of case study teaching fit into the picture? My reply is shown on the right side of Figure 1, where I suggest possible answers. I list the lecture case method as the weakest way to enhance learning using cases. The reason is because lecture cases are still lectures, albeit more interesting and entertaining than typical lectures. Lectures also do not stick in most students' minds for long.

Clicker cases, I predict, would fall about where lecture with visuals appears to fall because students are viewing a PowerPoint presentation and actively participating by clicking their answers to questions posed on the screen. In my classroom, I allow students to consult with their neighbors about their answers. Our recent studies comparing the lecture and clicker case methods support the superiority of the latter (Kang and others, 2009; Lundeberg and others, 2009; Wolter and others, 2011).

I have placed the discussion case method in the position of still greater retention than clicker cases because there is essentially no lecturing involved. The limitation of the discussion case method is that only one or a few students are engaged in a discussion with the instructor at any moment while the rest of the class is passive, unless the class, of course, is very small. Most of the couple of hundred studies that have been conducted on the use of clickers invariably claim that students enjoy using them in the classroom and that they learn more than in traditional classes. But there is an exception. Morgan (2008) reported no differences when clickers were used. In fact, students using clickers tended to be less engaged than in traditional small-discussion classes where everyone could directly engage with the professor. Morgan surmised that class size may be critical in determining the effectiveness of clickers. This finding may also be true for the effectiveness of discussion method in general; small might be better. This point needs further exploration.

Turning to the individual learning styles of case teaching, if we abide by the Cone of Learning, we are tempted to place them at the "Hands-on Independent Student Learning" level with 45 to 65 percent retention. This placement seems especially appropriate for the dialogue case method in which students independently research a topic and then write contrasting views in the form of a dialogue. It is less appropriate for the directed case method and the computer simulation "Case It" project, where the majority of the work is individual but there are general discussion or role-playing components.

I ranked the small-group case methods as the optimum approach for teaching. We expect the greatest retention when there is a maximum amount of interaction between participants, especially when students are teaching other students. In this category we find PBL, the interrupted case method, team learning, and intimate debate. In their original formats, PBL and team learning attempted to capture the strengths (e.g., improved critical thinking) of students working cooperatively in permanent groups. Faculty members customarily implement these methods as an entire package for a semester. They are less well suited for use in single classroom sessions.

In contrast, the intimate debate and interrupted case methods are ideal for single sessions. But because intimate debate is a specialized method appropriate for controversial topics and thus limited to special occasions, the interrupted case method is perhaps the most viable and exciting method for the majority of teaching occasions. In its pure form, the case is delivered one component at a time. Small groups of students wrestle with questions after each component and report their findings during a general discussion. If I had to rank the methods in terms of potential effectiveness, I would rank PBL and the interrupted case as the best of the small-group methods, because they engage students actively and directly in the puzzle-solving process.

Conclusion

Instructors obviously choose the technique that seems most appropriate for the situation at hand. Nonetheless, they should be aware that some types of case methods have a greater potential for learning than others. The model I have proposed provides a guide for such decisions. It will be a challenge to see how well this model stands up to experimental scrutiny in the future.

References

Allen, D. E., Donham, R. S., and Bernhardt, S. A. "Problem-Based Learning." In W. Buskist and J. E. Groccia (eds.), *Evidence-Based Teaching.* New Directions in Teaching and Learning. San Francisco: Jossey-Bass, 2011, *128.*

Barrows, H., and Tamblyn, R. *Problem-Based Learning: An Approach to Medical Education.* New York: Springer, 1980.

Bergland, M., and others. "Exploring Biotechnology Using Case Based Multimedia." *American Biology Teacher,* 2006, *68*(2), 81–86.

Chaudhury, S. R. "The Lecture." In W. Buskist and J. E. Groccia (eds.), *Evidence-Based Teaching.* New Directions in Teaching and Learning. San Francisco: Jossey-Bass, 2011, *128.*

Cliff, W., and Wright, A. "Directed Case Study Method for Teaching Human Anatomy and Physiology." *Advances in Physiology Education,* 1996, *270*(6), 19–28.

Dale, E. *Audio-Visual Methods in Teaching.* (3rd ed.) New York: Dryden Press, 1969.

Dochy, F., Segers, M., Van den Bossche, P., and Gijbels, D. "Effects of Problem-Based Learning: A Meta-Analysis." *Learning and Instruction,* 2003, *13,* 533–568.

Hake, R. "Interactive-Engagement versus Traditional Methods: A Six-Thousand-Student Survey of Mechanics Test Data for Introductory Physics Courses." *American Journal of Physics,* 1998, *66,* 64–74.

Herreid, C. "Case Studies in Science—A Novel Method of Science Education." *Journal of College Science Teaching,* 1994, *23,* 221–229.

Herreid, C. "Sorting Potatoes for Miss Bonner: Bringing Order to Case-Study Methodology Through a Classification Scheme." *Journal of College Science Teaching*, 1998, 27, 236–239.

Herreid, C. "The Interrupted Case Method." *Journal of College Science Teaching*, 2005a, 35, 4–5.

Herreid, C. "Using Case Studies to Teach Science." *American Institute for Biological Sciences*, 2005b. http://actionbioscience.org/education/herreid.html

Herreid, C. "Clicker Cases: Introducing Case Study Teaching into Large Classrooms." *Journal of College Science Teaching*, 2006, 36, 43–47.

Herreid, C. *Start with a Story: The Case Study Method of Teaching College Science.* Arlington, Va.: NSTA Press, 2007.

Herreid, C. F., and DuRei, K. "Intimate Debate: The Medicinal Use of Marijuana." *Journal of College Science Teaching*, 2007, 36, 10–13.

Johnson, D., and Johnson, R. *Cooperation and Competition: Theory and Research.* Edina, Minn.: Interaction Book Co., 1989.

Johnson, D., Johnson, R., and Smith, K. *Active Learning: Cooperation in the College Classroom.* Edina, Minn.: Interaction Book Co., 2006.

Kang, K., and others. "Giving Women a Voice and Making Science Relevant: Using Personal Response Systems ('Clickers') with Case Studies in Large Lecture Classrooms." Paper presented at the European Science Education Association, Istanbul, Turkey, September 2009.

Kay, R., and LeSage, A. "A Strategic Assessment of Audience Response Systems Used in Higher Education." *Australian Journal of Education Technology*, 2009, 25, 235–249.

Kim, S., and others. "A Conceptual Framework for Developing Teaching Cases: A Review and Synthesis of the Literature across Disciplines." *Medical Education*, 2006, 40, 867–876.

Lord, T. "Revisiting the Cone of Learning—Is It a Reliable Way to Link Instruction Method with Knowledge Recall?" *Journal of College Science Teaching*, 2007, 37, 14–17.

Lundeberg, M., and Yadav, A. "Assessment of Case Study Teaching: Where Do We Go from Here? Part I." *Journal of College Science Teaching*, 2006a, 35(5), 10–13.

Lundeberg, M., and Yadav, A. "Assessment of Case Study Teaching: Where Do We Go from Here? Part II." *Journal of College Science Teaching*, 2006b, 35(6), 8–13.

Lundeberg, M., and others. "Using Personal Response Systems ('Clickers') with Case Studies in Large Lecture Classes to Impact Student Assessment Performance: Which Cases Matter?" Paper presented at the annual meeting of American Educational Research Association, San Diego, California, April 2009.

Michaelsen, L., Knight, A., and Fink, L. *Team-Based Learning: A Transformative Use of Small Groups.* Westport, Conn.: Praeger, 2002.

Morgan, K. "Exploring the Pedagogical Effectiveness of Clickers." *Insight: Journal of Scholarly Teaching*, 2008, 3, 31–36.

Patry, M. "Clickers in Large Classes: From Student Perceptions towards an Understanding of Best Practices." *International Journal of the Scholarship of Teaching and Learning*, 2009, 3, 1–11.

Svinicki, M., and McKeachie, W. J. *McKeachie's Teaching Tips: Strategies, Research, and Theory for College and University Teachers* (13th ed.). Belmont, Calif.: Cengage, 2011.

Wolter, B.H.K., Lundeberg, M. A., Kang, H., and Herreid, C. F., with Armstrong, N., Borsari, B., Boury, N., Brickman, P., Hannam, K., Heinz, C., Horvath, T., Knabb, M., Platt, T., Rice, N., Rogers, B., Sharp, J., Ribbens, E., Hagley, R., Goulet, T., and Meier, K. "Students' Perceptions of Using Personal Response Systems ('Clickers') with Cases in Science." *Journal of College Science Teaching.* 2011, 40(4), 14–19.

Yadav, A., and others. "Teaching Science with Case Studies: A National Survey of Faculty Perceptions of the Benefits and Challenges of Using Cases." *Journal of College Science Teaching*, 2007, 37, 34–38.

CLYDE FREEMAN HERREID *is State University of New York distinguished teaching professor and director of the National Center for Case Study Teaching in Science at the University at Buffalo.*

5

In this chapter, we examine the relationship between the best practices of evidence-based teaching and the principles that constitute team-based learning.

Team-Based Learning

Larry K. Michaelsen, Michael Sweet

In *Evidence Based Teaching* (2006), Petty built on a great deal of educational research (for example, Bransford, Brown, and Cocking, 2000; Marzano, 1998; see also Hattie, 2009) to conclude that the six best practices in evidence-based teaching (EBT) are:

1. Cooperative learning
2. Feedback or "assessment for learning"
3. Reciprocal teaching
4. Whole-class interactive teaching
5. Requiring concept-driven decisions
6. Visual presentations and graphic organizers

Team-based learning (TBL), when properly implemented, includes many, if not all, of the common elements of these evidence-based best practices. To explain how, a brief overview of TBL is in order.

The four practical elements of TBL are:

1. Strategically formed, permanent teams
2. Readiness assurance
3. Application activities that promote both critical thinking and team development
4. Peer evaluation

(See Michaelsen, Knight, and Fink, 2004; Michaelsen, Parmelee, McMahon, and Levine, 2008.)

NEW DIRECTIONS FOR TEACHING AND LEARNING, no. 128, Winter 2011 © Wiley Periodicals, Inc.
Published online in Wiley Online Library (wileyonlinelibrary.com) • DOI: 10.1002/tl.467

Table 1. Typical TBL Unit

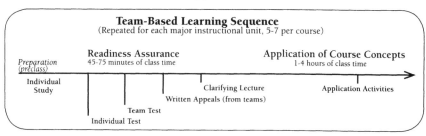

In brief, the rhythm of a TBL course works in this way: Students begin each unit of the course taking a short test over their understanding of the assigned prereadings. They then take that exact same test again as a team, getting immediate feedback on their team answers through the use of an Immediate Feedback Assessment (IF-AT) answer sheet. This immediate feedback reveals how well they thought and talked about the material and who among them may have the best grasp of it in the moment. Once the team test is completed, they can then write "appeals" to reclaim credit for incorrect answers when they feel they can cite evidence from the reading to make a case for their answer. After this readiness-testing experience, the teacher reviews the team scores to see which material is still unclear to the class and lectures briefly on that material. Students then complete one or more higher-level application exercises in which they apply what they learned during the readiness tests to complex problems or case studies. This process repeats for each unit of the course, with students filling out peer evaluations for members of their team a few times over the course of the term. A typical TBL unit is illustrated in Table 1.

By design, this sequence of activities shifts the focus of class time away from nearly 100 percent content "delivery" to students actively helping each other learn how to apply the content. Experience has shown that by increasing preclass teaching and peer instruction, TBL enables instructors to achieve equal or better content coverage and still use 70 to 80 percent of class time with students engaged in activities that deepen understanding of how course content applies to real-life situations and problems. In addition, TBL uses peer assessment and feedback both to increase team members' accountability to one another and to develop students' team problem-solving and decision-making abilities.

Four Essential Elements of TBL

Each of the four practical pillars of TBL can be implemented to make use of the best practices of evidence-based teaching.

Strategically Formed, Permanent Teams. Although the first essential element of TBL is strategically formed, permanent teams, TBL practitioners tend to be wary of being grouped with those who practice "cooperative learning." This wariness stems from the fact that, although both TBL and cooperative learning use small groups, there can be more differences than similarities in the way groups and group activities are managed. For example, cooperative learning techniques such as the jigsaw or constructive controversy are activities that can be dropped into an otherwise traditional, lecture-based course. TBL, however, is a comprehensive instructional system that, when implemented correctly, achieves an increasingly interlocking synergy and amplifies students' social and intellectual capacities over time.

However, using Petty's (2006) definitions, TBL very clearly qualifies as an example of cooperative learning. Specifically, Petty (p. 150) described the characteristics of cooperative learning as students sinking or swimming together, students working interactively, students having a goal to learn and a goal to help other students in their group, students learning how to cooperate effectively, and the teacher holding students accountable.

In TBL, the instructor organizes permanent teams of five to seven students in the first week or two of the term. Many of the differences between cooperative learning and TBL stem from the fact that all of the listed characteristics are much more apparent with strategically formed, permanent teams than with the temporary groups that are used for most applications of cooperative learning.

Readiness Assurance. After students have been organized into teams, each unit of the course begins with a four-step process called the readiness assurance process (RAP).

1. *Prereading by students outside of class.* This includes podcasts and other forms of media.
2. *Individual readiness assurance test (iRAT).* This is a short, basic, multiple-choice test about the preparation materials.
3. *Team readiness assurance test (tRAT).* Once students turn in their individual tests, they then take the exact same test again, and must come to consensus on their team answers. Importantly, teams *must* get immediate feedback on their performance, currently best achieved using scratch-off forms in the immediate feedback assessment technique (IF-AT).
4. *Appeals.* When teams feel they can make a case for their answers marked as incorrect, they can use their course materials to generate written appeals, which must consist of (a) a clear argumentative statement and (b) evidence cited from the preparation materials.

The RAP is followed by a clarifying lecture, in which the teacher targets information that the tRAT scores show students do not yet understand (for example, "All the teams got questions 1 to 5 correct, so that material

NEW DIRECTIONS FOR TEACHING AND LEARNING • DOI: 10.1002/tl

can be considered 'covered,' but questions 6 to 10 were hit and miss, so let me explain that material a bit more.")

The RAP makes use of several of EBT best practices, primarily *feedback* (assessment for learning) and the principles that underlie *reciprocal teaching*. The purpose of the RAP is not only to motivate students to come to class prepared but also to give them several experiences of feedback on their grasp of assigned material. The key to RAP's success is providing immediate feedback on the tRAT. Currently, immediate feedback is accomplished most often using cards that students scratch like lotto tickets (IF ATs), with the correct answer identified by a star. IF ATs give teams real-time feedback on every team decision and enable teachers to award partial credit when teams require more than one scratch to discover the correct answer. (See Figure 1.)

The benefit of the IF AT is that it provides many rounds of low-stakes, formative feedback in a very short period of time. What may be not so obvious is the extent to which the tRAT stimulates students to interact in much the same way as they would in a formal reciprocal teaching situation. In their search for correct answers, students invariably alternate in and out of a teacher's role by asking each other the kinds of questions that the teacher normally would ask. For example, on any given question, students might ask each other to make predictions, explain their rationales for those predictions, and clarify their different understandings of the material. This interaction pattern is illustrated by an excerpt from a recorded transcript during a tRAT in an undergraduate educational psychology class (Sweet and Pelton-Sweet, 2009, p. 36).

Student 4: I put A.
Student 6: Well, I'd go with A. I put D but—
Student 1: I put D too, but . . .
Student 2: I put D.
Student 3: I put D, but . . .
Student 4: Well!
[group laughter]

Figure 1. Immediate Feedback Technique (IF-AT) Form

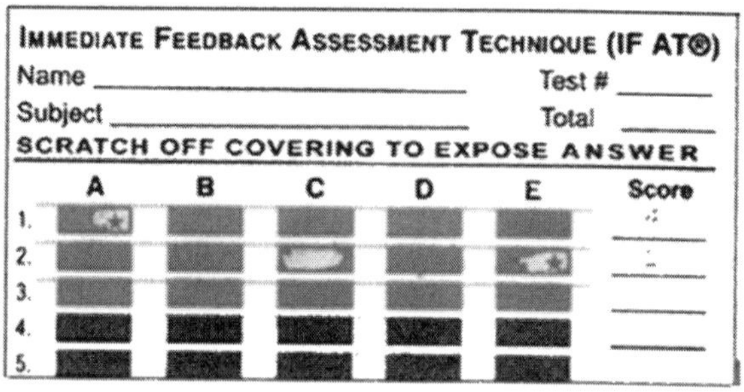

Student 4: Well, then someone argue for D and then someone argue for A, and we'll figure it out.

Student 6: I don't even have a good argument.

Student 1: It just seems more logical to me, that's all. D sort of seems more logical, but . . .

Student 4: Yeah, I just, I remember reading A and not D. That's the only thing why I would not change it.

Student 1: Yeah, if you remember reading it. I would be willing to trust your reading it more than my logic.

Student 6: Yeah, we're just trying to justify it.

In this excerpt, Student 4 was not assigned to play the role of the teacher—TBL pointedly does *not* recommend the assignment of group roles—but she briefly assumed the teacher's role by proposing an inquiry-based task to the group: "Someone argue for D and then someone argue for A, and we'll figure it out." In the next few statements, students evaluated their confidence in the sources of their opinions ("I would be willing to trust your reading it more than my logic") with Student 6 even stating that the purpose of this exercise is that "we're just trying to justify it." Although these particular statements do not fall crisply into the categories of predicting, summarizing, and clarifying as prescribed by the formal regimen of reciprocal teaching, they nonetheless structure the interaction and help students coregulate one another's learning in much the same way by alternating teacher and student roles.

After the RAP, the teacher is prepared to deliver, and students are eager to receive, a highly targeted clarifying lecture. The teacher can look at team scores on the RATs and say, for example, "Every team got questions 1 to 5 correct. That material has been covered." Students either learned it from the readings or taught it to each other. When teams struggle with a particular concept, the instructor is able to engage in "whole class interactive teaching" (Petty, 2006) because, at this point, students have been *primed* by feedback on the RAP to listen actively and zero in on exactly the parts of the content they do not understand. At this point the teacher can do one of two things. The ideal strategy is to conduct a class discussion in which teams that correctly answered challenging questions can explain their answers. The other strategy is that, when students' explanations are inadequate, the teacher can deliver a straight-up corrective and/or explanatory lecture.

4-S Application Activities. Having completed the RAP and received whatever clarifying, whole-class interactive teaching was required, teams then apply the knowledge they have acquired to carefully designed 4-S application activities. These activities work best when they require teams to:

1. Address a **Significant problem** that demonstrates a concept's usefulness.

2. Make a **Specific choice** among clear alternatives (for example, Which of these is the *best* example of X? What is the *most* important piece of evidence in support of Y? With which statement would the author *most* agree?).

3. Work on the **Same problem** as other teams, so each team will care about the conclusions and rationales of the other teams.

4. **Simultaneously report** their decisions, so differences among teams can be explored for the optimal instructional effect. Some of the most common approaches for simultaneous reporting include having students:

   a. Hold up lettered and/or colored cards that correspond to specific choices.

   b. Record a short answer on an index card and display their cards simultaneously on a document camera.

   c. Write their choices on flip-chart paper and simultaneously post them for review and critique by other teams (for example, see the concept map in Figure 2).

Although the details of implementing 4-S application activities are unique based on factors such as subject matter and class size, 4-S's are wholly consistent EBT best practices. For example, because all 4-S activities require teams to make specific decisions, even though not all of them involve a card-sorting game, they can be said to employ a general form of the "Decisions, Decisions" learning structure (Petty, 2006). That said, some 4-S applications do involve sorting cards. For example, King (2010) distributed cards with pictures of an infant in various positions and required

Figure 2. Representative Concept Map Generated by TBL Teams

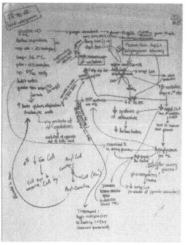

		Most relevant	Few relevant
Content	All relevant concepts are included and are correct	concepts and mechanisms are included and are correct	facts or concepts are included or correct
Points	6 5	4 3	2 1
Logic and understanding	Understanding of facts and concepts is clearly demonstrated by correct links and active verbs	Understanding of facts and concepts is demonstrated but with some incorrect links and/or missing active verbs	Poor understanding of facts and concepts with significant errors in links and active verbs
Points	6 5	4 3	2 1
Presentation	Concept map is neat, clear, legible, has easy-to-follow links, and has no spelling errors	Concept map is neat, legible but with some links difficult to follow and some spelling errors	Concept map is untidy with links difficult to follow and spelling errors
Points	3	2	1

teams to sort them according to various criteria—the most basic being normal or abnormal (for example, when lying on their backs, infants of a certain age should habitually face forward and keep their head centerline to their body; dropping their heads and looking to one side or another is a sign of abnormal development).

Similarly, many teachers use 4-S application activities that require teams to complete graphic organizers or concept maps, thereby implementing the EBT practice of visual presentations or graphic organizers. For example, Restad, Onion, Reynolds, and Sweet (2010) had teams fill out "argument templates" that required them not only to gather evidence from the readings, but also use that evidence to take a stand on a given statement. An example is shown in Table 2.

Table 2. Argument Template Example

The McCarthy Era: What Were the Fears? How Real Were the Fears?

I. WHAT FEARS DO EACH OF THE FOLLOWING PRIMARY SOURCE DOCUMENTS CALL INTO PLAY?

Be as precise as possible in describing each of the fears.

Source	Specific fears
A. "Duck and Cover"	
B. *Communism*	
C. "Hiss and Chambers"	
D. "Is This Tomorrow"	

II. THE BEST EVIDENCE. Rank the "sources" 1 (strongest) – 4 (weakest) in response to each of these statements:
1. The most balanced and reputable information about the early Cold War period
2. The most useful for understanding era

Source	1. most balanced	2. most useful
A		
B		
C		
D		

III. HISTORICISM versus PRESENTISM
Referring to the above documents, the readings, and your knowledge of Cold War events, agree or disagree with the following statement. Write a short (no more than 25 words) justification for your answer that reflects the team's best "history essay" style.
"The hysteria and restriction of civil liberties during the Cold War was justified."

AGREE / DISAGREE

NEW DIRECTIONS FOR TEACHING AND LEARNING • DOI: 10.1002/tl

Another popular form of visualizing TBL course content is to ask teams to generate concept maps in response to a given prompt. For example, Thompson, LeClair, Winterson, and Manyan (2010) received the concept map shown in Figure 2 from a team diagramming the primary and secondary biochemical effects in the case of an eighteen-month-old infant with medium-chain acyl-coenzyme A dehydrogenase deficiency. Teams then critiqued one another's concept maps with different colors representing primary and secondary effects. Then teams critiqued each other using the rubric shown to the right.

Application activities can be graded or ungraded and need not have a "correct" answer. Although it may seem difficult to grade a concept visualization, Thompson and others (2010) developed an elegant rubric with which to grade team-generated concept maps.

Once teams produce their decisions—either in simple form by holding up cards indicating A, B, C, D or producing more complex output, such as a graphic organizer or concept map—the teacher again has the opportunity for a rich round of whole-class interactive teaching. The fact that students can see each other's specific choices in relation to the same problem, they are both prepared and motivated to challenge each other's choices and defend their own. As a result, the teacher need only invite the teams to inquire about each other's rationales to begin what will inevitably be a content-rich class discussion that he or she will typically conclude by confirming the points that students have already made and adding his or her own insights and/or providing corrective instruction when it is needed.

Peer Evaluation. Peer evaluation is the fourth and final practical element of TBL, providing students with both formative and summative feedback from their teammates about their contributions to the team and its success. Whereas members of a group feel mostly accountable to an outside authority, team members also feel accountable to each other, and peer evaluation is a mechanism by which the teacher can stimulate that experience in one's students.

As Petty (2006) noted, the format of feedback is important so that it is informative and not judgmental. Therefore, many TBL teachers have students fill out peer evaluation forms that ask them to express things they "appreciate" about their teammates and things they "request" (see Table 3). This language is carefully chosen so as not to stimulate attacks or judgments but instead promote constructive peer feedback. Students submit these forms to the teacher, who then processes the feedback and e-mails it to each student. Because the teacher knows who said what to whom, the feedback tends to be civil and constructive. However, because students do not know the specific source of the comments they receive, team members are more likely to be honest in giving negative feedback when it is called for.

Table 3. Sample TBL Feedback Form

Team Reflection and Feedback   Team#_____   Name_____

To help your team become more effective, give your teammates some <u>anonymous</u> feedback.
Consider such things as:

- *Preparation:*   Were they prepared when they came to class?
- *Contribution:* Did they contribute to the team discussion and work?
- *Gatekeeping:*   Did they help <u>others</u> contribute?
- *Flexibility:*   Did they listen when disagreements occurred?

You have 25 points to distribute among your teammates. These are anonymous, so be honest. :-)

1. Team Member Name:	Points
Things I appreciate about this team member: *Things I would like to request of this team member:*	
2. Team Member Name:	Points
Things I appreciate about this team member: *Things I would like to request of this team member:*	

. . .

Evidence for the Effectiveness of TBL

One strong, although indirect, set of evidence for the effectiveness of TBL is the extremely close fit between TBL and virtually all of the prescriptions common to the best practice approaches identified by Petty (2006). In fact, in many cases, TBL goes beyond the specific prescriptions in ways that promote consistency *across* the entire set of the best practice approaches. For example, a common practice of "Decisions, Decisions" involves assigning students to specific roles to ensure differences of opinion as they attempt to reach a decision that affects multiple parties. By contrast, TBL creates differences of opinion by using 4-S application assignments that require students to make decisions about what they think is the best answer to a highly complex problem and then have their choices immediately challenged by other teams that have reached a different conclusion.

TBL benefits students in three ways.

1. The positions they are defending are truly authentic.
2. Consistent with all best practice approaches, as long as they do not get

discouraged and give up, students learn more as the questions they face become more difficult.

3. Because TBL explicitly harnesses the power of real teams, teachers are able to provide decision tasks that would be overwhelming for individual students and that are too difficult for most learning groups.

Given the consistency between TBL and EBT best practices, it is not surprising that TBL produces a wide range of positive outcomes. Since initial studies nearly thirty years ago (for example, Wilson, 1982), the volume of literature about TBL's effectiveness has accumulated across a wide variety of disciplines in dozens of countries worldwide and has grown too large to be well summarized here. The best we can do in this limited space is to describe the breadth of the landscape across which TBL has been found to produce positive results. To date, empirical studies of TBL have reported increased test performance (Koles, Stolfi, Borges, Nelson, and Parmelee, 2010), attendance/engagement (Shankar and Roopa, 2009), retention (Wilson, 1982), student attitudes toward group work (Clark, Nguyen, Bray, and Levine, 2008), student satisfaction with their learning experience (Beatty and others, 2009), and coregulated learning (aka team "synergy") (Watson, Michaelsen, and Sharp, 1991). In addition, because of increasing use of TBL and its focus on active student engagement and outcomes achievement, several schools using TBL have been cited as promoting exemplary teaching practice by visiting teams from their respective accreditation agencies (S. Doscher, personal communication, 2010; M. Sinclair, personal communication, 2010). The two best sources for a more complete listing of empirical studies of TBL are the bibliography at the online Team-Based Learning clearinghouse (www.teambasedlearning.org) and Wright State University's database of medical education TBL scholarship (www.med.wright.edu/aa/facdev/tbl/ArticleAppl.htm).

References

Beatty, S. J., and others. "Team-Based Learning in Therapeutics Workshop Sessions." *American Journal of Pharmacy Education*, 2009, 73, 100.

Bransford, J. D., Brown, A. L., and Cocking, R. R. (eds.). *How People Learn: Brain, Mind, Experience and School*. Washington, D.C.: National Academies Press, 2000.

Clark, M. C., Nguyen, H. T., Bray, C., and Levine, R. E. "Team-Based Learning in an Undergraduate Nursing Course." *Nursing Education*, 2008, 47, 111–117.

Hattie, J. *Visible Learning: A Synthesis of over 800 Meta-Analyses Relating to Achievement*. New York: Routledge, 2009.

King, M. P. "Successful Application Exercises: Charting Data and Image Sorting for an Intra-Professional Group of Graduate Nursing Students." Poster presented at the annual meeting of the Team-Based Learning Collaborative, New Orleans, Louisiana, March 2010.

Koles, P. G., Stolfi, A., Borges, N. J., Nelson, S., and Parmelee, D. X. "The Impact of Team-based Learning on Medical Students' Academic Performance." *Academic Medicine*, 2010, 85(11), 1739–1745.

Marzano, R. J. *A Theory-based Meta-Analysis of Research in Instruction* (Technical Report). Aurora, Colo.: Midcontinent Regional Educational Laboratory, 1998. (ERIC Document Reproduction No. ED 427087.)

Michaelsen, L. K., Knight, A. B., and Fink, L. D. *Team-Based Learning: A Transformative Use of Small Groups in College Teaching.* Sterling, Va.: Stylus, 2004.

Michaelsen, L. K., Parmelee, D. X., McMahon, K. K., and Levine, R. E. (eds.). *Team-Based Learning for Health Professions Education: A Guide to Using Small Groups for Improving Learning.* Sterling, Va.: Stylus, 2008.

Petty, G. *Evidence Based Teaching.* Gloucestershire, U.K.: Nelson-Thornes, 2006.

Restad, P., Onion, R., Reynolds, A., and Sweet, M. "Doing History with Team-Based Learning in a Large Survey U.S. History Course." Poster presented at the annual meeting of the Team-Based Learning Collaborative, New Orleans, Louisiana, March 2010.

Shankar, N., and Roopa, R. "Evaluation of a Modified Team Based Learning Method for Teaching General Embryology to 1st Year Medical Graduate Students." *Indian Journal of Medical Science,* 2009, *63,* 4–12.

Sweet, M., and Pelton-Sweet, L. M. (2009). "The Social Foundation of Team-Based Learning: Students Made Accountable to Students." In L. K. Michaelsen, M. Sweet, and D. X. Parmelee (eds.), *Team-Based Learning: Small Group Learning's Next Big Step.* New Directions for Teaching and Learning, no. 116. San Francisco: Jossey-Bass.

Thompson, K. H., LeClair, R. J., Winterson, B. J., and Manyan, D. R. "Concept Mapping as a Team-Based Learning Application Exercise in a First-Year Medical Biochemistry Course." Poster presented at the annual meeting of the International Association of Medical Science Educators, New Orleans, Louisiana, July 2010.

Watson, W. E., Michaelsen, L. K., and Sharp, W. "Member Competence, Group Interaction and Group Decision-Making: A Longitudinal Study." *Journal of Applied Psychology,* 1991, *76,* 801–809.

Wilson, W. R. "The Use of Permanent Learning Groups in Teaching Introductory Accounting." Unpublished Doctoral Dissertation, University of Oklahoma, 1982.

LARRY K. MICHAELSEN *is professor of management at the University of Central Missouri and David Ross Boyd professor emeritus at the University of Oklahoma.*

MICHAEL SWEET *is director of instructional development for the Center of Teaching and Learning at the University of Texas, Austin.*

This chapter describes a new behavior-analytic teaching method called interteaching and the growing body of research showing that interteaching is more effective than traditional teaching methods.

Interteaching

Bryan K. Saville, Tracy E. Zinn

In general, people associate college and university teaching with lecture-based methods (Benjamin, 2002), in which an expert (the teacher) delivers information to a group of nonexperts (the students), who subsequently show their newfound "knowledge" by answering examination questions. Because of the common notion that knowledge and intelligence are traits that students "possess," many teachers believe that their job is simply to distribute important information to a captive audience. From there, it is the students' responsibility to learn the information as best they can. In this view, lectures are simply a medium for information dissemination, and the onus for learning falls squarely on students. Unfortunately, lecture-based methods that serve as the cornerstone of pedagogy in the U.S. educational system tend to be relatively ineffective at improving student learning (Benedict and Anderton, 2004; Dochy, Segers, Van de Bossche, and Gijbels, 2002; Halpern and Hakel, 2003; Kulik, Kulik, and Cohen, 1979; Saville and others, 2006; Tiwari, Lai, So, and Yuen, 2006; but see Chaudhury, this volume). More and more, teachers are becoming aware of the ineffectiveness of lecture-based teaching. As a result, many are seeking alternatives that improve student learning and enjoyment.

Where should teachers start if they want to introduce more effective teaching methods into their classrooms? Although some teachers might be tempted to search the teaching literature in hopes of finding a handful of activities that they could quickly incorporate into class, we suggest a slightly different approach. We believe that teachers should examine what researchers already know about human learning and then seek out teaching methods that are based on well-established psychological models. In this

NEW DIRECTIONS FOR TEACHING AND LEARNING, no. 128, Winter 2011 © Wiley Periodicals, Inc.
Published online in Wiley Online Library (wileyonlinelibrary.com) • DOI: 10.1002/tl.468

chapter, we describe interteaching, a relatively new teaching method that has its roots in one of these models.

Behavior Analysis and Education

Throughout the history of psychology, many models for understanding behavior and learning have emerged from laboratory-based research. One of the oldest and best known of these models is based on the early work of E. L. Thorndike and B. F. Skinner. From his classic studies, Thorndike (1911) concluded that events following an individual's behavior exert profound effects on whether that behavior will occur again. According to Thorndike's law of effect, behavior resulting in a satisfying state of affairs will become more frequent, whereas behavior resulting in an annoying state of affairs will become less frequent. Skinner (1938, 1953) later revised and expanded the tenets of the law of effect, resulting in his well-known operant psychology or, as it is known today, behavior analysis. Since Thorndike's and Skinner's pioneering studies, the law of effect and the basic tenets of behavior analysis have provided a way for psychologists to understand and modify socially important behaviors (Baer, Wolf, and Risley, 1968; Cooper, Heron, and Heward, 2007).

Beginning in the 1950s, Skinner ([1954], 1999) and others began focusing their efforts on developing educational tools based on well-known behavioral principles. In line with Skinner's notions about the causes of behavior, behavioral educators believed that restructuring the classroom environment was imperative for enhancing student learning and enjoyment (see Moran and Malott, 2004). Throughout the late 1960s and 1970s, behavior-analytic teaching methods, the most well known of which was Keller's (1968) personalized system of instruction (PSI), gained popularity and became the pedagogy of choice for many college instructors (Keller, 1974; Kulik, Kulik, and Carmichael, 1974; Kulik and others, 1979). The systematic examination of behavioral teaching methods also blossomed during this time, with many studies showing that behavioral methods produced better student learning outcomes than more traditional methods. (For a review, see Moran and Malott, 2004.)

Despite these positive research outcomes, PSI and other behavioral teaching methods failed to gain widespread popularity and ultimately lost favor with college instructors. Buskist, Cush, and DeGrandpre (1991) suggested two reasons for their demise.

1. Because lecture-based methods have been around for so long, college instructors prefer them simply because that is how they learned in college.
2. The prevailing structure of most educational settings makes it difficult to introduce alternative methods that do not fit nicely into this general scheme. For instance, introducing a truly self-paced system (as Keller

NEW DIRECTIONS FOR TEACHING AND LEARNING • DOI: 10.1002/tl

intended PSI to be) into a traditional fifteen-week semester might lead to administrative headaches.

Thus, despite the fact that behavioral teaching methods produced increases in student learning and enjoyment, they no longer occupy an important position in the pedagogical toolkits of most college instructors.

Interteaching

In response to concerns about the utility of behavioral teaching methods, Boyce and Hineline (2002) introduced interteaching. In its original conception, interteaching included several components:

- Preparation (prep) guides
- Pair discussions
- Record sheets
- Participation points
- Clarifying lectures
- Frequent tests
- Quality points

Next we briefly describe how interteaching works (see also Saville, Lambert, and Robertson, 2011).

Before each class period, the instructor provides students with a prep guide that contains questions regarding an assigned reading. Usually the questions are factual, conceptual, or applied in nature and require students to connect material from different parts of the course or with material from other courses. Typically, the instructor requires that students complete the prep guides before class and be prepared to discuss the answers with a partner during class.

Once in class (and following a brief lecture), students pair up with one another to discuss their prep-guide answers. Although Boyce and Hineline (2002) discussed different configurations, they suggested using pairs rather than larger groups to avoid situations where one individual does not participate in the conversation. During the pair discussion, the teacher (and teaching assistants, if available) circulates among the students, answering questions and facilitating discussion, and thus becomes privy to a large sample of student behavior. By using pair discussions and mingling with different groups, the instructor develops a clear understanding of students' level of comprehension of course material.

Following pair discussion, students complete a record sheet on which they list their and their partner's names, evaluate discussion quality, and note which topics were difficult to understand. The instructor then compiles this information and constructs a lecture for the next class period.

NEW DIRECTIONS FOR TEACHING AND LEARNING • DOI: 10.1002/tl

The instructor can also use the record sheets to assign participation points, which Boyce and Hineline (2002) recommended should be worth 10 percent of each student's total course grade.

At the start of the next class period, the instructor discusses the questions that students listed most frequently on the record sheets. The lectures last about one-third of the class period and focus on those topics that students found most difficult to comprehend; the instructor might also include supplementary information during the lectures. Once the lecture is finished, students pair off and discuss the next prep guide.

Boyce and Hineline (2002) also recommended frequent assessments (i.e., five or six tests per semester), which should cover material from both prep guides and lectures. The tests might contain one or more essay questions taken directly from prep guides, other objective questions (e.g., multiple choice, short answer) derived from important concepts, and questions that require students to apply the concepts they learned. The purpose of the tests is to evaluate students on behaviors they practiced while completing prep guides and participating in discussions.

Finally, Boyce and Hineline (2002) suggested using *quality points* to encourage effective pair discussions. Quality points, which Boyce and Hineline suggested should be worth 10 percent of students' course grades, work in this way. If two students discussed a prep guide in class and an essay question from that prep guide appeared on the test, the quality points each student receives are partially dependent on the other's performance. For example, if both students earned an A or B on a particular question (e.g., 4 or 5 points on a 5-point question), both students would earn quality points toward their course grades. If, however, either or both students earned less than a B on that question (i.e., fewer than 4 points), neither would earn quality points. Because students' grades are partially dependent on the performances of their discussion partners, it is in the students' best interests to help each other learn the material as effectively as possible.

Capitalizing on Established Learning Principles

"Learning" refers to relatively permanent changes in behavior brought on by experience. Thus, if students learn, they are able to behave in ways they could not before, as, for instance, correctly answering questions about E. L. Thorndike or anything else they might be taught during their lives. Many teaching formats focus on dispensing information and then rely on students to learn that information by reviewing it frequently. Unfortunately, the frequent studying that would be beneficial when a student has only three tests in a semester is usually maintained by long-term, relatively weak contingencies, such as getting a good grade at the end of the semester (Michael, 1991). But with interteaching, the instructor modifies the classroom environment to promote behaviors that will likely lead to learning—behaviors such as attending class, studying consistently, and discussing important course material. Interteaching produces these behaviors in several ways.

Interteaching requires students to work in pairs rather than in small groups. Because a conversation requires the participation of at least two people, students quickly learn that coming to class unprepared produces negative social consequences, both from discussion partners, who find it unpleasant when their partners have nothing to say, and from the teacher, who can listen to the discussions and identify which students are unprepared. Thus, students are likely to complete their prep guides and ready themselves to discuss the material before class. Implementing a point system for completing pair discussions likely increases the chances that students will attend class and thus participate in the pair discussions.

In most lecture classes, students listen and take notes, often copying verbatim from PowerPoint slides. Many times the behavior required of students on tests, though, is more complicated. On tests, students usually have to connect concepts, elaborate on ideas, synthesize information, and show they can apply principles to solve problems. It is precisely these behaviors that students practice with interteaching when answering prep-guide questions and participating in pair discussions. By practicing these behaviors during class, students are well prepared to behave appropriately (i.e., answer questions correctly) on exams.

The lecture in an interteaching classroom is also different from that in most lecture classes. Rather than preceding desired behaviors such as studying and discussing course material, interteaching lectures follow these behaviors. As a result, students are well prepared to participate during lectures. Because the instructor is reviewing material that students requested, students also are more likely to remain interested in the lecture. In sum, interteaching puts in place contingencies that are likely to produce effective studying behaviors.

Research on Interteaching

Although Boyce and Hineline (2002) introduced a teaching method based on well-established behavioral principles and provided anecdotal evidence in support of its efficacy, they did not provide systematic data. In the first experimental analysis of interteaching, Saville, Zinn, and Elliott (2005) conducted a laboratory-based study in which they randomly assigned undergraduate psychology students to one of four teaching conditions: an interteaching condition, a reading condition, a lecture condition, and a control condition. One week later, the students returned to the lab to take a ten-question, multiple-choice quiz. Saville and colleagues found that students in the interteaching condition correctly answered a significantly greater percentage of questions than students in the other conditions. They also found that students' quiz performance in the reading and lecture conditions was statistically indistinguishable from students' quiz performance in the control condition.

In a subsequent pair of studies, Saville and others (2006) compared interteaching to lecture in two different college courses. In Study 1, students in a graduate-level special education course took pretests over course material before the start of the semester. They then experienced alternating weeks of interteaching and lecture, each of which ended with a posttest over the material. Overall, the differences between pretest and posttest scores were greater after interteaching sessions than they were after lecture sessions. A majority of students also reported that they preferred interteaching to lecture. In Study 2, the researchers alternated several times between interteaching and lecture in two sections of an undergraduate research methods course, equally alternating (counterbalancing) the order of presentation across sections. After each unit of material, students in both sections took the same exam. Students exposed to interteaching always had higher exam scores than students in the lecture condition, with an average difference of about 10 percentage points across all six exams. In addition, a majority of students in both sections preferred interteaching to lecture.

Scoboria and Pascual-Leone (2009) compared interteaching to lecture in several large sections of an undergraduate abnormal psychology course. They assessed student performance on writing activities designed to measure critical and analytical thinking and also asked students to report on satisfaction with interteaching. Students exposed to the interteaching method showed higher levels of critical and analytical thinking than students who took a lecture-based version of the same course (see also Saville and others, 2008). Most students also preferred interteaching to lecture.

Goto and Schneider (2010) examined the efficacy of interteaching in an upper-level undergraduate nutrition course (see also Goto and Schneider, 2009). Although Goto and Schneider did not directly compare interteaching to lecture, they did ask students to think about their experiences in lecture-based courses when evaluating the efficacy of interteaching. Students in the interteaching course reported high levels of class preparation, critical thinking, and motivation. They also reported that interteaching gave them a sense of responsibility for teaching others and produced better learning than traditional lectures.

Researchers have also begun to conduct analyses to determine which components of interteaching contribute to its effectiveness. Saville and Zinn (2009) examined whether the quality-points component of interteaching affected exam performance of students in two sections of an undergraduate general psychology course. Students in both sections participated in interteaching, but Saville and Zinn alternated between awarding quality points and no quality points several times during the semester, counterbalancing the order of presentation across sections. They found no significant difference between sections on five of the six exams and concluded that the quality-points contingency was likely too delayed to have an impact on the behaviors that indicated student learning.

Cannella-Malone, Axe, and Parker (2009) subsequently examined whether different types of prep-guide construction affected exam performance in an undergraduate special education course. Specifically, these researchers wanted to know whether the seven students in the course would do better on quizzes when they constructed their own prep-guide questions or when they completed instructor-prepared prep guides. Although they found that overall quiz scores were not significantly different across conditions, they did find that writing questions produced slightly higher scores by the end of the semester. They also found that students performed differently on particular types of quiz questions. On multiple-choice and problem-solving, short-answer questions, students did better if they had written their own prep-guide questions, but on fill-in-the-blank and factual, short-answer questions, students did better when they completed the instructor-prepared prep guides.

Conclusion

Interteaching is a new pedagogical method that has its roots in well-established behavioral principles. For teachers wishing to incorporate evidence-based teaching methods into their classrooms, interteaching might be a welcome alternative to the traditional lecture-based methods that have continued to define college and university teaching. Although the number of studies on interteaching is small, the results have been promising. For this reason, we hope that researchers will continue to study interteaching more systematically and that teachers will consider implementing this potentially promising alternative in their classrooms.

References

Baer, D. M., Wolf, M. M., and Risley, T. R. "Some Current Dimensions of Applied Behavior Analysis." *Journal of Applied Behavior Analysis*, 1968, *1*, 91–97.
Benedict, J. O., and Anderton, J. B. "Applying the Just-in-Time Teaching Approach to Teaching Statistics." *Teaching of Psychology*, 2004, *31*, 197–199.
Benjamin, L. T., Jr. "Lecturing." In S. F. Davis and W. Buskist (eds.), *The Teaching of Psychology: Essays in Honor of Wilbert J. McKeachie and Charles L. Brewer* (pp. 57–67). Mahwah, N.J.: Lawrence Erlbaum, 2002.
Boyce, T. E., and Hineline, P. N. "Interteaching: A Strategy for Enhancing the User-Friendliness of Behavioral Arrangements in the College Classroom." *Behavior Analyst*, 2002, *25*, 215–226.
Buskist, W., Cush, D., and DeGrandpre, R. J. "The Life and Times of PSI." *Journal of Behavioral Education*, 1991, *1*, 215–234.
Cannella-Malone, H. I., Axe, J. B., and Parker, E. D. "Interteach Preparation: A Comparison of the Effects of Answering versus Generating Study Guide Questions

on Quiz Scores." *Journal of the Scholarship of Teaching and Learning*, 2009, *9*, 22–35.

Chaudhury, S. R. "The Lecture." In W. Buskist and J. E. Groccia (eds.), *Evidence-Based Teaching. New Directions in Teaching and Learning*. San Francisco: Jossey-Bass, 2011, 128.

Cooper, J. O., Heron, T. E., and Heward, W. L. *Applied Behavior Analysis*. (2nd ed.) Upper Saddle River, N.J.: Pearson, 2007.

Dochy, F., Segers, M., Van de Bossche, P., and Gijbels, D. "Effects of Problem-Based Learning: A Meta-Analysis." *Learning and Instruction*, 2002, *13*, 533–568.

Goto, K., and Schneider, J. "Interteaching: An Innovative Approach to Facilitate University Student Learning in the Field of Nutrition." *Journal of Nutrition Education and Behavior*, 2009, *41*, 303–304.

Goto, K., and Schneider, J. "Learning Through Teaching: Challenges and Opportunities in Facilitating Student Learning in Food Science and Nutrition by Using the Interteaching Approach." *Journal of Food Science Education*, 2010, *9*, 31–35.

Halpern, D. F., and Hakel, M. D. "Applying the Science of Learning to the University and Beyond." *Change*, 2003, *35*(4), 36–42.

Keller, F. S. "Good-bye Teacher . . ." *Journal of Applied Behavior Analysis*, 1968, *1*, 79–89.

Keller, F. S. "Ten Years of Personalized Instruction." *Teaching of Psychology*, 1974, *1*, 4–9.

Kulik, J. A., Kulik, C., and Carmichael, K. "The Keller Plan in Science Teaching." *Science*, 1974, *183*, 379–383.

Kulik, J. A., Kulik, C. C., and Cohen, P. A. "A Meta-Analysis of Outcome Studies of Keller's Personalized System of Instruction." *American Psychologist*, 1979, *34*, 307–318.

Michael, J. "Behavioral Perspectives on College Teaching." *Behavior Analyst*, 1991, *14*, 229–239.

Moran, D. J., and Malott, R. W. (eds.). *Evidence-Based Educational Methods: Advances from the Behavioral Sciences*. New York: Academic Press, 2004.

Saville, B. K., Lambert, T., and Robertson, S. "Interteaching: Bringing Behavioral Education into the 21st Century. *Psychological Record*, 2011, *61*, 153–166.

Saville, B. K., and Zinn, T. E. "Interteaching: The Effects of Quality Points on Exam Scores." *Journal of Applied Behavior Analysis*, 2009, *42*, 369–374.

Saville, B. K., Zinn, T. E., and Elliott, M. P.   "Interteaching versus traditional methods of instruction: A preliminary analysis." *Teaching of Psychology*, 2005, *32*, 161–163.

Saville, B. K., and others. "A Comparison of Interteaching and Lecture in the College Classroom." *Journal of Applied Behavior Analysis*, 2006, *39*, 49–61.

Saville, B. K., and others. "Teaching Critical Thinking in Statistics and Research Methods." In D. S. Dunn, J. S. Halonen, and R. A. Smith (eds.), *Teaching Critical Thinking in Psychology: A Handbook of Best Practices* (pp. 149–160). Malden, Mass.: Wiley-Blackwell, 2008.

Scoboria, A., and Pascual-Leone, A. "An 'Interteaching'-Informed Approach to Instructing Large Undergraduate Classes." *Journal of the Scholarship of Teaching and Learning*, 2009, *9*, 29–37.

Skinner, B. F. *The Behavior of Organisms: An Experimental Analysis*. New York: Appleton-Century-Crofts, 1938.

Skinner, B. F. *Science and Human Behavior*. New York: Free Press, 1953.

Skinner, B. F. "The Science of Learning and the Art of Teaching. *Harvard Educational Review*, 1954, *24*, 86–97. (Reprinted in B. F. Skinner, *Cumulative Record, Definitive Edition*, pp. 179–191 [Cambridge, Mass.: B. F. Skinner Foundation, 1999]).

Thorndike, E. L. *Animal Intelligence*. New York: Macmillan, 1911.

Tiwari, A., Lai, P., So, M., and Yuen, K. "A Comparison of the Effects of Problem-Based Learning and Lecturing on the Development of Students' Critical Thinking." *Medical Education,* 2006, *40,* 547–554.

BRYAN K. SAVILLE *is an associate professor in the Department of Psychology at James Madison University.*

TRACY E. ZINN *is an associate professor in the Department of Psychology at James Madison University.*

7

This chapter provides an overview and implementation guidelines of Just-in-Time Teaching, an interactive engagement pedagogy used across disciplines and across the academy, now in its fourteenth year. The pedagogy has proven effective in improving classroom climate, student motivation and fostering deeper learning.

Just-in-Time Teaching

Gregor M. Novak

Tell me and I forget. Teach me and I remember. Involve me and I learn.
—Chinese proverb as quoted by Benjamin Franklin

At Indiana University, David Pace teaches a course titled *Visions of the Future: A History*. To promote productive participatory class time with engaged students, he asks his students to ponder a preparatory question and respond to him electronically shortly before coming to class. For example:

Imagine that you were preparing to write an essay in response to this question:

The development of new types of futures in the late 19th and early 20th century science fiction represented a major break with the kinds of visions of the future that had dominated Western culture since the triumph of Christianity in the Roman Empire. The grand moral perspectives that had characterized older Western futures were replaced by adolescent fantasies that had no higher purpose than attracting an audience.

A. Describe in your own words what this question is asking you to do.
B. From the three choices below identify the position you would take, if you were actually answering the question.
   1. The quotation is essentially correct, and I would present evidence to convince my readers of that fact.

NEW DIRECTIONS FOR TEACHING AND LEARNING, no. 128, Winter 2011 © Wiley Periodicals, Inc.
Published online in Wiley Online Library (wileyonlinelibrary.com) • DOI: 10.1002/tl.469

2. The quotation is essentially incorrect, and I would present evidence to convince my readers of that fact.

3. The quotation is partially correct and partially incorrect, and I would present evidence to convince my readers of that fact.

C. Very briefly present three bits of evidence that you would use to support your position and explain after each how it would make your case more plausible.

David Pace practices Just-in-Time Teaching (JiTT), a pedagogical technique used across the academy (Simkins and Maier, 2009). Note the main features of Pace's JiTT preclass warm-up:

1. The teacher provides students with a slightly provocative and memorable statement that is open to a considerable amount of interpretation.

2. Students' first task is to rephrase the question in their own words—the responses will tell the teacher how students interpret the assignment.

3. Students must take a stand and justify it—they must examine prior knowledge, consult course resources, and perhaps discuss the issue with classmates. All this intellectual activity happens *before* any formal classroom instruction.

JiTT Basics

The heart of JiTT pedagogy is Web-based pre-instruction assignments called warm-ups, with some colorful local variations, such as GeoBytes in a geology class (Guertin, Zappe, and Kim, 2007). Students respond to the warm-up questions and go to class with genuine interest and desire to learn the answers. The questions are a bit vague, open to interpretation, and, when fully explored, require fairly complex answers. Typically, students approach these questions with limited prior knowledge. Their responses form the foundation on which they eventually build a more complete understanding, possibly approaching that of an expert on the subject. Students submit responses online just a few hours before class, giving the teacher just enough time to incorporate insights gained from students' responses into the upcoming lesson. Exactly how the classroom time is used depends on a variety of issues, such as type of course, class size, classroom facilities, and student and teacher personalities.

Teachers and students become a teaching-learning team, ready to begin the lesson with an awareness of the mental status of the class, making the learning experience as relevant as possible to a particular class at a particular time. What happens in the classroom consists of a mix of preplanned activities and creative improvisation suggested by student responses and guided by students' in-class reactions to thoughts and opinions in those responses.

NEW DIRECTIONS FOR TEACHING AND LEARNING • DOI: 10.1002/tl

Over the fourteen-year evolution of JiTT, practitioners have enriched the practice, borrowing eclectically from many current learning theories and instructional techniques (Bransford, Brown, and Cocking, 2000). Particularly relevant is research into the ways students learn by weaving new knowledge into existing knowledge (Scott, Asoko, and Driver, 1991) and research that concerns itself with students' motivational beliefs and with the effects that classroom contextual factors have on learning (Beghetto, 2004).

JiTT is a Web-based pedagogy, but it definitely is not distance learning or computer-aided instruction. All JiTT instruction occurs in a classroom with human teachers. The Web materials, added as a pedagogical resource, act as a communication and organizing tool. Because much of the students' learning occurs outside the classroom, JiTT practitioners view their pedagogical strategy as feedback loops between teaching and learning and between in-class and out-of-class experiences.

Student–student and student–teacher interactions and time on task, the top three critical factors contributing to success in college (Astin, 1997), are enhanced immensely by technology. Timely Web assignments prepare students and instructors for subsequent in-class interaction, give students some control over their learning, and enrich in-class meetings.

Implementing JiTT Successfully

A JiTT-based course differs from a traditional lecture-based course in two significant aspects. First, having completed the Web assignment, students enter the classroom with a good start into the learning process. The teacher, having read the responses, also has a good sense of the state of the class. A profound effect can come when instructors change the way they think about their own teaching and, more important, about how their students' learn (Simkins and Maier, 2009).

This preparatory process makes the unknown unknowns into known unknowns, to paraphrase Donald Rumsfeld.

Second, starting the lesson this way invites students to assume some of the ownership of the process. Because student responses to a well-posed JiTT question are presented for the live classroom discussion, at least a part of the interactive lesson features students' own words.

There is much flexibility in constructing and using JiTT assignments. The variety across the disciplines is mutually enriching (Simkins and Maier, 2009). However, all implementations of JiTT satisfy two criteria:

1. Faculty thoughtfully construct assignments based on validated education research.
2. Student responses constitute an integral part of the lesson, not merely an add-on.

NEW DIRECTIONS FOR TEACHING AND LEARNING • DOI: 10.1002/tl

JiTT encourages *all* students in the course to:

- Participate in and reflect on the learning and teaching process.
- Appreciate perspectives other than their own.
- Apply concepts as they learn them.
- Connect these to other parts of the course, other courses, and the wider world.

JiTT encourages teachers to:

- Show interest in the useful mistakes students make and offer corrective support.
- Model how to learn from mistakes.
- Allow multiple attempts at learning tasks without severe penalties.
- Give credit for making progress in learning course content, not just for completed work.
- Foster a community for mutual help, which involves students and the teacher in a team effort.

Developing a JiTT Lesson. Preparing a lesson for any JiTT-based course typically follows five steps.

Step 1. JiTT teachers should think about the lesson content and the lesson type. Is it an introduction to a new topic or a continuation? Is the primary purpose of the lesson to explore conceptual issues or to develop and practice procedural skills? Does it involve laboratory or field work? Is it a comprehensive review?

Step 2. JiTT teachers should identify the lesson parts. Does the topic involve a single concept or multiple concepts? Is a review necessary? Will it include demonstrations or hands-on activities? How are the parts to be sequenced? How much time is to be devoted to each part?

Step 3. JiTT teachers should list any new concepts (words, definitions, examples.) If mathematics is involved, they should list the prerequisite skills and equations.

Step 4. JiTT teachers should design a set of questions that probe for the understanding or misunderstanding of the concepts. If the lesson is part of a sequence, the teacher should design questions that require application of knowledge acquired in previous lessons. Ideally, the question set is broad enough to enable construction of the lesson content from student responses. Teachers should anticipate potential student responses. When the submissions are in hand, the teacher should look for well-articulated versions of the arguments they anticipated as well as for surprise responses.

Step 5. Using the anticipated responses as a guide, JiTT teachers should outline the lesson flow but be flexible enough for surprises.

After all, it is difficult, if not impossible, to anticipate all possible student responses.

A good JiTT question is broad enough to elicit individual idiosyncratic student responses to enrich the classroom discussion. It requires an answer that cannot be looked up easily, and it encourages students to examine their prior knowledge and experience. The question demands that students formulate responses, including the underlying concepts, in their own words and is ambiguous enough to require that they supply some additional information not explicitly given in the question. (This feature enriches the subsequent classroom discussion. Grappling with the preclass questions prepares students for a discussion of complex, possibly controversial topics.)

JiTT questions can be constructed to help students deal with jargon and academic language. Formal academic language can be a serious barrier to deeper learning (Snow, 2010). In many subjects, dry definitions of technical terms and complex concepts leave students disinterested and often perplexed and confused. For example, consider this question:

Please explain in your own words what a focal point is, without referring to any particular device.

—From Andy Gavrin, Indiana University–Purdue University Indianapolis (IUPUI)

Pre-instruction questions may also explicitly encourage reflection and metacognition. For example:

Explain in simple terms how you solved warm-up #1. In particular, what questions did you ask yourself and what conclusions did you draw from the answers?

—From Bob Blake, Texas Tech University

In addition to disciplinary education research literature, many theory-based resources are useful when preparing a JiTT lesson. For example, Bransford and others' (2000) well-known treatise, *How People Learn: Brain, Mind, Experience, and School*, provides a good starting point. Also helpful is the literature related to Bloom's taxonomy and learning styles issues. For example, you may wish to consult resources such as the Baxter Magolda (1992) student maturity scale, Arons's (1979) list of student reasoning skills that may not be up to par, and the Middendorf–Pace Decoding the Disciplines Cycle Inventory (Middendorf and Pace, 2004).

After Student Submissions Have Been Collected. Student responses typically fall into a fairly well-defined set of categories that I have found useful for organizing and incorporating them into my lectures.

1. *Select representative examples for class discussion and weave them into the lesson.* Make sure that all students get their day in class by using each student's response at least once per lesson.
2. *Do not ignore free-form comments.* Every assignment should provide space for student comments, which very often yield valuable pedagogical insight into student thinking.
3. *Revise the lesson flow when you have actual responses.* The fact that the wording actually comes from the students makes the lesson fresh and interesting to them.
4. *Go to class and be ready to improvise if necessary.* The phrasing used in class will now come directly from student responses and will vary from class to class. The lesson flow is influenced by feedback from the live class. Each class session is unique because students in each class are unique.

Student classroom participation will be enhanced if students come to class with informed opinions that they are eager to share and defend (for example, Pace's question cited earlier).Good questions create a need to know in students, and should be sufficiently captivating so that even unmotivated students may become interested in the answers. For example:

> Allison is driving with her parents when they get in a serious car accident. At the emergency room, her doctor tells Allison that her mother, Carla, is fine, but her father Bob has lost a lot of blood and will need a blood transfusion. Allison volunteers to donate blood, and you tell her that her blood type is AB. Bob is type O. (a) Can Allison donate blood to Bob? Why or why not? (b) Allison, who is a biology student, begins to wonder if she is adopted. What would you tell her and why?
>
> **—From Kathy Marrs, IUPUI**

Adapting JiTT to One's Teaching Style

JiTT has to be adapted to one's teaching style, not just blindly adopted as a teaching technique. It has become clear that there is no such thing as canonical JiTT, no one-size-fits-all method. Just as we demand that students construct their own version of the subject matter, interactive engagement pedagogies demand that teachers construct their own brand of teaching tactics. Faculty reactions from JiTT classrooms range from euphoria to despair, largely dependent on whether they approached JiTT as a set of recipes or adapted it to match their teaching style and nature of the course.

When first attempting to implement JiTT, teachers should be prepared for a trial-and-error period while they adapt existing JiTT materials and create new ones. Teachers should also be sensitive to students' ideas, attitudes, and knowledge and should constantly monitor their learning progress. Of course, teachers should also have a good grasp of the material and have a repertoire of conceptual pathways to deliver and explain that material such that they can both appreciate and respond to students' ideas. Finally, effective JiTT teachers also have to be able to develop creative tasks that support students' learning within a classroom climate in which they may participate freely without the experience degenerating into frustrating chaos.

JiTT Demands on Students

When teachers first introduce JiTT to their students, students may find it difficult to work in the small, daily installments required by the drumbeat of the warm-ups. Thus, it is important that some enforcement mechanism be in place. Teachers have to hold students responsible for on-time delivery of meaningful responses. At least a part of the preclass assignment should include a free-form written response. Teachers should give credit for thoughtful, thorough responses, well reasoned from stated prior knowledge and assumptions, even if the responses are wrong. Teachers should encourage students to indicate the thought processes that led them to the response, as in Pace's example described earlier.

It also is important to help students to see that "wrong" answers are not evidence of failure on their part but are stepping-stones in the exploratory learning process. In fact, in the best JiTT classes, there are no "wrong" answers to the warm-up questions. What teachers expect of students, and reward, is evidence of thinking. Each discipline will experience its own version of this issue. For example, in the sciences, many students hold the positivist view that science is a compendium of incontrovertible facts; thus, they may be reluctant to consider their own or other students' perspectives in developing their answers to the warm-up questions or in discussing the questions in class. Scott and others (1991) suggested that deeper and more permanent learning occurs when teachers create a learning environment, teaching strategies, and learning tasks that foster conceptual change rather than piecemeal accretion of new information. To that end, JiTT teachers ask students to examine and evaluate their own points of view and those of other students.

Can JiTT Make a Difference in Student Learning?

In JiTT, the word "assessment" connotes many ideas. JiTT assignments are themselves a form of assessment. They continuously provide a sight line into students' progress toward deeper learning. However, in addition to monitoring cognitive gains, it is necessary to pay attention to the affective aspects of students' involvement in the course. Successful implementation of the JiTT strategy depends critically on total teacher and student buy-in. If students see the online assignments merely as an add-on to the course, to be completed perfunctorily in the shortest time possible and then discussed briefly at the beginning of class, before the "real" lecture, they will resent the extra work and will not get any additional benefit from JiTT. Teachers using JiTT report a spectrum of results, ranging from significant affective and cognitive gains to very negative student reactions, disillusionment, and sometimes a regression in learning gains (Camp as cited in Simkins and Maier, 2009).

Cognitive Gains. Successful JiTT implementations lead to cognitive gains ranging from moderate to quite significant. For example, in a first-semester introductory physics course, the standard assessment instrument is the Force Concept Inventory (FCI), wherein identical multiple-choice questions are administered on the first and last days of class. Improvement, if any, is measured in terms of the "Hake gain" defined as (posttest percent − pretest percent)/(100 − pretest; Hake, 1998). Typical improvement scores in traditional courses are in the teens; however, JiTT practitioners report gains in the 40 to 70 percent range (Hake, 1998). The gains are even stronger when JiTT is paired with other interactive engagement techniques, such as peer instruction or collaborative learning (Crouch and Mazur, 2001).

Another interesting result comes from a five-semester study at North Georgia College & State University (Formica, Easley, and Spraker, 2010). This study analyzed responses from FCI questions (the distracters as well as the correct answers) for evidence of students developing "Newtonian thinking" skills, a well-defined notion in physics education (Arons, 1979; Hestenes and Halloun 1995). Sixty-one percent of students in the JiTT class reached the threshold, compared with only 7 percent of students in the traditionally taught class.

Marrs reported similar gains on pre–post assessment in biology, using the Hake rubric (Marrs as cited in Simkins and Maier, 2009). With traditional lecture-based pedagogy, the gain was 16.7 percent. In a class using JiTT or collaborative learning, the gain jumped to 52.3 percent with JiTT and to 63.6 percent with collaborative learning.

Since the introduction of JiTT at the U.S. Air Force Academy, final exam questions in the introductory physics sequence have shifted significantly toward conceptual probing for deeper understanding. Analyzing carefully kept records from the pre-JiTT early 1990s until the present, one finds that despite the increasingly more challenging questions, scores have held steady and even improved in some semesters. In this example, there are too many variables in play to make this case into a rigorous piece of evidence, but most physics teachers looking at these data would likely be impressed by the depth of thinking required by the Air Force cadets in JiTT courses.

Classroom Climate, Motivation, and Attitude. When we introduced JiTT in introductory physics at IUPUI in 1996, course attendance jumped from under 50 percent to over 80 percent. Instructors in other disciplines have reported similar results. Better attendance inevitably leads to fewer students dropping the class and an overall rise in grades. In JiTT physics and biology courses at IUPUI, the percentage of D/F/W grades plunged from 40 percent to under 25 percent.

Warm-ups can make a difference in student study skills. Students in Marrs's biology class credit JiTT for a significant decrease in cramming for tests (Marrs as cited in Simkins & Maier, 2009). She asked her students "Did you put off studying for Biotech 540 and as a result 'cram' for Biotech 540 tests?" to her graduate students, and 34 percent answered yes. However, 62 percent of the class answered in affirmative to the question "Do you 'cram' for other courses that you have this semester?"

Gavrin reported that 80 percent of the students in his JiTT class responded "yes" to "Do the JiTT exercises help you to be well prepared for lecture?" versus 21 percent affirmative to the same question in "other classes." He found a 58 percent versus 18 percent split on "staying focused," a 59 percent versus 18 percent split on "feeling like an active participant," and a 71 percent versus 21 percent split on "finding classroom time useful" (Gavrin as cited in Simkins & Maier, 2009).

Student comments on the free-form climate question, included in most JiTT assignments, show a similar trend. Students complain about the assignments being "time consuming," but they usually recognize the benefits. For example, a student in Gavrin's JiTT class commented, "[T]hey are a pain, but they help me prepare" (Gavrin as cited in Simkins & Maier, 2009, p. 127).

Conclusion

When trying to assess the efficacy of any pedagogical strategy, it is important to appreciate that the choice and implementation of a particular teaching method will affect student and faculty attitudes and motivation as well as learning outcomes. In her use of JiTT, Laura Guertin has noticed strongly positive reactions from her students:

> I see my students working weekly through open-ended questions that require higher-order cognitive skills. I see students working together in class, gaining additional practice with quantitative, communication, and management skills. I see my students using the vocabulary of the discipline as they work through JiTT exercises and discuss JiTT responses in class. I see students connecting ideas across the course and across their lives. (quoted in Simkins & Maier, 2009, p. 111)

We have much anecdotal evidence that, in the best of cases, after adopting student-centered teaching approaches such as JiTT, many faculty members change their teaching philosophies, sometimes in significant ways. Faculty members who once viewed their role as being "conveyors of knowledge" shift to becoming "facilitators of student learning." This developmental shift increases the efficacy of subsequent teaching and ultimately increases "deep learning" experienced by students.

However, as is the case with all innovations in teaching and learning, further questions remain to be answered by scholarly work. For example, with respect to JiTT:

How do we define what "working" actually means when we ask if JiTT is working?

What factors determine how much "resistance" students will show when first introduced to JiTT?

What types of JiTT questions/problems are most effective in helping students master the material at a deeper level?

What skills do students develop in JiTT courses that they do not develop, or not develop as well, in non-JiTT courses?

Do students retain knowledge longer in JiTT courses compared with non-JiTT courses?

Undoubtedly, answers to these questions will lead to a better understanding of how JiTT impacts student learning and, just as important, of faculty teaching effectiveness.

References

Arons, A. B. "Some Thoughts on Reasoning Capacities Implicitly Expected of College Students." In J. Lockhead and J. Clemens (eds.), *Cognitive Process Instruction: Research on Teaching and Learning Skills* (pp. 209–215). Philadelphia: Franklin Institute Press, 1979.

Astin, A. W. *What Matters in College?: Four Critical Years Revisited.* San Francisco: Jossey-Bass, 1997.

Baxter Magolda, M. B. *Knowing and Reasoning in College: Gender-Related Patterns in Students' Intellectual Development.* San Francisco: Jossey-Bass, 1992.

Beghetto, R. A. "Toward a More Complete Picture of Student Learning: Assessing Students' Motivational Beliefs." *Practical Assessment, Research and Evaluation*, 2004, 9(15). http://PAREonline.net/getvn.asp?v=9&n=15

Bransford, J. D., Brown, A. L., and Cocking, R. R. (eds.). *How People Learn: Brain, Mind, Experience, and School.* Washington, D.C.: National Academies Press, 2000.

Crouch, C. H., and Mazur, E. "Peer Instruction: Ten Years of Experience and Results." *American Journal of Physics*, 2001, 69, 970–977.

Formica, S. P., Easley, J. L., and Spraker, M. C. "Transforming Common-Sense Beliefs into Newtonian Thinking through Just-in-Time Teaching." *Physical Review Special Topics—Physics Education Research*, 2010, 6. http://prst-per.aps.org/abstract/PRSTPER/v6/i2/e020106

Guertin, L. A., Zappe, S. E., and Kim, H. "Just-in-Time Teaching (JiTT) Exercises to Engage Students in an Introductory-Level Dinosaur Course." *Journal of Science Education and Technology*, 2007, 16, 507–514.

Hake, R. R. "Interactive-Engagement versus Traditional Methods: A Six-Thousand-Student Survey of Mechanics Test Data for Introductory Physics Courses." *American Journal of Physics*, 1998, *66*, 64–74.

Hestenes, D., and Halloun, I. "Interpreting the Force Concept Inventory: A Response to Huffman and Heller." *Physics Teacher*, 1995, *33*, 502–506.

Middendorf, J., and Pace, D. (eds.). *Decoding the Disciplines. Helping Students Learn Disciplinary Ways of Thinking*. New Directions for Teaching and Learning, no. 98. San Francisco: Jossey-Bass, 2004.

Scott, P. H., Asoko, H. M., and Driver, R. H. "Teaching for Conceptual Change: A Review of Strategies." In R. Duit, F. Goldberg, and H. Niederer (eds.), *Research in Physics Learning: Theoretical Issues and Empirical Studies. Proceedings of an International Workshop Held at the University of Bremen* (pp. 310–329). Kiel: Institute for Science Education, 1991. IPN 131. http://scholar.google.com/scholar?q=related:knI7UIQcwp IJ:scholar.google.com/&hl=en&as_sdt=0,15

Simkins, S., and Maier, M. (eds). *Just-in-Time Teaching across the Disciplines and across the Academy*. Sterling, Va.: Stylus, 2009.

Snow, C. E. "Academic Language and the Challenge of Reading for Learning about Science." *Science*, 2010, *328*, 450–452.

GREGOR M. NOVAK *is distinguished scholar in residence in the Center for Physics Education Research at the United States Air Force Academy and professor emeritus of physics at Indiana University–Purdue University Indianapolis.*

NEW DIRECTIONS FOR TEACHING AND LEARNING • DOI: 10.1002/tl

This chapter defines service-learning and reviews the evidence regarding its academic, civic, personal, and other learning outcomes. Although service-learning produces positive outcomes in many areas, the pedagogy's most significant outcome may be the transformative learning that can result for all participants.

Service-Learning

Peter Felten, Patti H. Clayton

Institutions of higher education institutions in the United States have always had public as well as academic purposes. The earliest colleges aimed to prepare religious and civic leaders for colonial communities. Thomas Jefferson and others conceived of universities as cultivating capacities for self-governance. The 1862 Morrill Act created land-grant colleges to make higher education widely accessible and thereby enhance the nation's economic, technological, and civic development. This theme echoes in contemporary calls for institutions of higher education to become more engaged with broader communities and to focus on the education of young people as citizens (Boyer, 1996; Bringle, Games, and Malloy, 1999; Colby and others, 2003; Saltmarsh and Hartley, 2011).

The question of how best to fulfill the academy's role in civic life animates many discussions about the identity and function of higher education in the twenty-first century. Service-learning is emerging as a central component of efforts to connect both disciplinary learning and general education with this historic and increasingly salient commitment to public purposes. *Educating Citizens: Preparing America's Undergraduates for Lives of Moral and Civic Responsibility* (2003) by Colby and others and "How Civic Engagement Is Reframing Liberal Education" (2003) by Rhoads are but two influential calls for conceptualizing teaching and learning in ways that connect campus with community. Building on this renewed emphasis, in 2006, the Carnegie Foundation launched an elective "Community Engagement" classification that highlights curricular integration of civic with academic learning.

New Directions for Teaching and Learning, no. 128, Winter 2011 © Wiley Periodicals, Inc.
Published online in Wiley Online Library (wileyonlinelibrary.com) • DOI: 10.1002/tl.470

Service-learning is embraced as both a mechanism for community engagement and high-impact pedagogy across institution types and disciplines and at undergraduate and graduate levels. For example, the Series on Service-Learning in the Disciplines includes volumes for over twenty fields. Recent years have also seen growth in research on service-learning, including the establishment of the peer-reviewed *Michigan Journal for Community Service Learning* in 1994 and of the annual International Research Conference on Service-Learning and Community Engagement in 2000. The evidence base on the impact of service-learning, and on the design variables that shape its outcomes, continues to expand and deepen.

Defining, Designing, and Implementing Service-Learning

Since Sigmon's foundational article "Service-Learning: Three Principles" (1979) formalized the pedagogy, numerous definitions of service-learning have emerged. Ehrlich (1996) provided a general framework:

> Service-learning is the various pedagogies that link community service and academic study so that each strengthens the other. The basic theory of service-learning is Dewey's: the interaction of knowledge and skills with experience is key to learning. (p. xi)

Bringle, Hatcher, and McIntosh (2006) offered perhaps the most cited operational definition:

> Service-learning is a course-based, credit-bearing educational experience in which students (a) participate in an organized service activity that meets identified community needs and (b) reflect on the service activity in such a way as to gain further understanding of course content, a broader appreciation of the discipline, and an enhanced sense of personal values and civic responsibility. (p. 12)

As the field has matured, the range of definitions has converged on several core characteristics. Service-learning experiences:

- Advance learning goals (academic and civic) and community purposes
- Involve reciprocal collaboration among students, faculty/staff, community members, community organizations, and educational institutions to fulfill shared objectives and build capacity among all partners
- Include critical reflection and assessment processes that are intentionally designed and facilitated to produce and document meaningful learning and service outcomes

Within these parameters, service-learning experiences vary based on local context and the objectives and constraints of those involved. Service-learning courses range across the curriculum, from first-year surveys to

NEW DIRECTIONS FOR TEACHING AND LEARNING • DOI: 10.1002/tl

graduate seminars. Service-learning experiences include short-term modules, semester-long activities, and multiyear as well as multicourse projects. The service may be direct or indirect, may involve low or high levels of responsibility, and may have a research component. "Community" may be construed as on-campus, in the local neighborhood, in a nearby municipality, in another state or country, or online. The term may refer to one or more partners, from small grassroots initiatives to large nonprofit or for-profit organizations. Reciprocity is essential to the collaboration between community and campus, creating a strong connection between the academic context and public concerns. Reflection enables and reinforces this linkage. Reflection may take written and/or oral forms, may be undertaken individually and/or collaboratively, and may occur with varying degrees of frequency and feedback. Critical reflection is the component of service-learning that generates, deepens, and documents learning (Ash and Clayton, 2009a, 2009b).

Service-learning experiences can be understood and designed through the lens of a simple conceptual framework shown in Figure 1. As this model illustrates, service-learning aims to develop academic knowledge/skills/dispositions as well as civic learning and personal growth—either of which may be defined to include such widely valued outcomes as intercultural competence and teamwork. Developing critical-thinking skills is often an explicit goal, as is learning at the intersections of the categories.

The interdependence of learning processes and outcomes with community processes and outcomes not only renders service-learning powerful as a vehicle for learning and social change, but also makes it challenging to implement effectively. As one example of this complexity, community organizations are not mere learning laboratories but rather realms of significant problem solving and human interaction, which means that much more than student learning is at stake. With its interdisciplinary, experiential, reflective, nonhierarchical, and unpredictable nature, service-learning is among the most "counternormative" of pedagogies, by design deviating in significant ways from traditional teaching and learning strategies with which students and faculty alike may well be more familiar (Clayton and Ash, 2004; Howard, 1998). Among other implications, the range and nature of evidence regarding its impact—and how we go about generating and documenting that evidence—is in some ways familiar and in other ways nontraditional.

Review of the Empirical Evidence

As summarized by Eyler (2010), "A good deal is now known about the impact of service learning on students' outcomes and on the particular characteristics of service learning that affect specific types of results" (p. 225). Her review of research to date confirms "a fairly consistent pattern of small but significant impact . . . on college students' personal, academic,

Figure 1. Conceptual Framework for Service-Learning

Components of Service-Learning

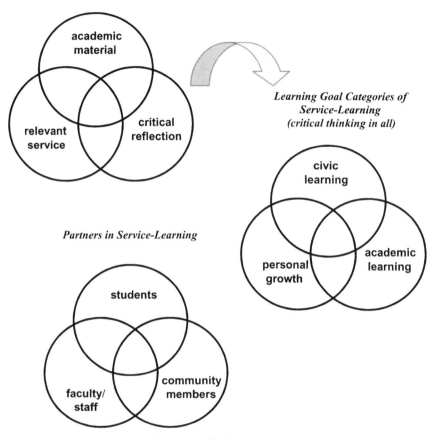

Learning Goal Categories of Service-Learning (critical thinking in all)

Partners in Service-Learning

Source: Reprinted with permission from Ash and Clayton, 2009b.

and social outcomes . . . and growing evidence of . . . impact on behavior and civic engagement" (p. 225).

In 2008, the Association of American Colleges and Universities published Kuh's report on *High-Impact Educational Practices*. This analysis drew on years of data collected through the National Survey of Student Engagement (NSSE), supplemented by other research, to identify educational practices that "are correlated with positive educational results for students from widely varying backgrounds" (p. 1). NSEE relies on students' reports of their experiences and takes as a reasonable proxy for learning various well-established indicators of "engagement," such as close faculty–student interaction (Carini, Kuh, and Klein, 2006). Service-learning correlates strongly with deep learning and personal development for both first-year and senior-level undergraduates (the populations targeted by NSSE). Significantly, "historically underserved students tend to benefit *more*" from engaged pedagogies, like service-learning, than majority students do, although these practices are "high-impact" for *all* types of students (Kuh, 2008, p. 17).

A frequently cited investigation of service-learning's outcomes (Astin, Vogelgesang, Ikeda, and Yee, 2000) included a mix of quantitative and qualitative methods to generate longitudinal data from over 22,000 undergraduates on campuses across the United States. Some students participated in service-learning, some in community service, and some in neither. The authors examined the impacts of community service and service-learning in several areas including academic performance, values, self-efficacy, leadership, career plans, and intention to engage in service after graduation. Participation in community service was correlated with significant positive results in all areas examined, with service-learning outcomes further enhanced on all measures except self-efficacy and leadership. The strongest service-learning outcomes appeared in the category of academic performance, and the most significant factors influencing academic outcomes were student preparation for service, reflection, and subject-matter interest, which the authors suggested indicates the value of using the pedagogy in major courses. The authors concluded that in well-designed service-learning activities, students are prompted to evaluate differing perspectives and complex situations, which can lead to development of their capacity to think critically and to understand social issues.

In another influential study, Eyler and Giles (1999) used pre– and post–problem-solving interviews to gather evidence about various aspects of student reasoning, including the application of knowledge in new situations. This study revealed that "participation in well-integrated and highly reflective service-learning courses was a predictor of increased complexity in analysis of both causes and solutions to social problems" (p. 75). Drawing on cognitive theory to help explain the pedagogy's ability to promote intellectual growth, the authors suggested that service-learning encourages students to consider perspectives other than their own and helps them cultivate capacities for making informed judgments.

Researchers have found it more challenging to authentically assess specific disciplinary learning associated with the pedagogy. Eyler and Giles (1999) contended that traditional measurements, especially of factual knowledge and other lower-level learning goals, might not adequately capture service-learning's most significant contributions to students' academic development. Direct comparisons of student learning in service-learning and non–service-learning courses in fields as disparate as child development (Strage, 2000), composition (Wurr, 2002), and rehabilitation services (Mpufo, 2007) demonstrate consistent patterns. Service-learning did not appear to enhance factual knowledge as measured, for example, by standard exams—students in service-learning sections performed comparably to their traditionally taught peers on those measures. However, on higher-order thinking tasks, such as analytical essays and case-based assignments, students in service-learning sections consistently performed better than their peers. Reviewing these and other studies, Jameson, Clayton, and Ash (forthcoming) noted that service-learning appears to contribute to equivalent basic knowledge acquisition but enhanced critical thinking within disciplinary contexts. They also explored and called for research on the pedagogy's role in cultivating student capacities to think from disciplinary and interdisciplinary perspectives.

Ash, Clayton, and Atkinson (2005) reinforced the emerging consensus that service-learning is particularly well suited to cultivate higher-order reasoning and critical thinking with a study that examined iterations across time of student reflection products. The curricular context for the study included careful guidance of student reflection to support the integration of service-learning experiences with academic (and other) learning objectives. The level of students' reasoning about disciplinary concepts as measured with two rubrics—one based on Bloom's (1956) taxonomy and the other on Paul and Elder's (2006) standards of critical thinking—increased over time, although not so significantly as their thinking in the categories of civic learning and personal growth. This study confirmed the central role of well-integrated critical reflection and suggested that students may require scaffolding and guided practice to move beyond application of course concepts to, for example, critical evaluation of those concepts. Students often may need to learn how to learn through critical reflection, and doing so helps develop their capacities for higher-order reasoning and critical thinking.

Evidence for service-learning's civic learning outcomes is compelling. A large study (Astin and others, 2006) following students at more than 200 institutions from their first year in college to six years after graduation demonstrated that service-learning and other community-based experiences contribute to long-term student political and community involvement, especially when supported by faculty-led reflection. Eyler (2010) summarized the findings of several major studies comparing students who participated in service-learning with those who did not, reporting that service-learning contributed to political interest and efficacy, a sense of connectedness to community, social responsibility, future intent to participate in community life, and life skills. Pascarella and Terenzini (2005) claimed the evidence is "conclusive" (p. 304) that service-learning contributes to enhanced civic engagement.

More than two decades of research also provides consistent evidence that "service-learning has a positive effect on student personal development" (Eyler, Giles, Stenson, and Gray, 2001, p. 1). As summarized by Brandenberger (forthcoming), personal growth outcomes that have been investigated include sense of efficacy, spiritual development, identity formation, self-authorship, moral development, agency, career development, leadership, and well-being. Service-learning often exposes students to people and experiences that are new to them, potentially leading to openness to diverse perspectives and ways of being (Fitch, 2005; Jones and Abes, 2004) as well as enhanced empathy (Lundy, 2007). For example, multiple studies (Astin and others, 2000; Kahne and Westheimer, 2006; Stewart, 2009) suggested that service-learning contributes to significant gains in self-efficacy, although Pascarella and Terenzini (2005) posit that service-learning experiences may prompt students to understand more fully the true complexity of social problems and thereby cause them to lose previously held, often naïve, confidence in their individual capacity to effect systematic change.

Key to many of these outcomes is the way in which service-learning evokes integrated cognitive and affective responses. In service-learning, students often come face-to-face with troubling social realities, making connections between emotion and learning, a particularly salient consideration for this pedagogy. Building on Dewey's ([1933], 1997) theorizing about the central role of dissonance in learning, service-learning practitioner-scholars have begun to explore the positive roles emotion can play in learning, emphasizing how the emotional dimensions of experience can contribute to developmental outcomes, including enhanced motivation, empathy, and persistence (Felten, Gilchrist, and Darby, 2006).

Conclusion: Service-Learning's Transformative Potential

Generic conclusions regarding the effectiveness of service-learning or any other pedagogy are less meaningful than critical determination of the conditions under which it is effective in producing specified types of outcomes. Our synthesis of the research suggests that service-learning is most effective at generating significant educational outcomes in these cases:

- Learning and service goals are appropriate and integrated.
- Student work is designed so that goals, experiences in the community and in the classroom, reflection activities, and assessment are aligned and complementary.
- The community partnership is collaborative throughout, from initial planning to completion.
- The experience is integrative, bridging what students do in and out of class and connecting perspectives and knowledge from the full range of participants.
- The pedagogy is intentionally designed yet flexible enough to accommodate dynamic situations and to respond to capacity-building needs and opportunities for everyone involved.

Underlying these design characteristics is a set of epistemological commitments that give service-learning its unique power to cultivate wide-ranging and deep outcomes. Fundamentally, service-learning challenges the traditional identities and roles of students and calls on them not only to consume knowledge but also to produce it. Given the associated radical shifts it evokes, well-designed service-learning can facilitate significant transformation of student perspectives and practices (Clayton and Ash, 2004), providing what Eyler and Giles (1999) called a "new set of lenses for seeing the world" (p. 129) and new ways of being in it. Such "transformative learning" (Cranton, 2006; Mezirow and Associates, 2000) occurs when learners change their frames of reference by critically reflecting on their assumptions, beliefs, and understanding of the world.

Service-learning also holds the potential for such transformational outcomes because it fosters what Vandenberg (1991) referred to as the capacity to engage with others "as 'cobeings' and not as objects" (p. 1281). Reciprocal, authentic relationships—such as those that underlie service-learning at its best—provide conditions well suited to transformative learning. Several practitioner-scholars (e.g., Jameson, Clayton, and Jaeger, 2010; Saltmarsh, Hartley, and Clayton, 2009) posit that service-learning's potential is maximized when it positions students, faculty, and community members as co-learners, coeducators, and cogenerators of knowledge. Thus, unlike much other pedagogy, the defining learning outcomes of service-learning transcend students to encompass learning and development for everyone involved. The claim of former service-learning student leaders that "ultimately, students best undertake [service-learning as] a developmental journey when those who support and mentor them are also striving for growth through the same process" (Whitney, McClure, Respet, and Clayton, 2007, p. 195) is a powerful argument for intentionally cultivating the full range of learning outcomes across all partners and for gathering evidence based on service-learning's mutually transformative potential.

References

Ash, S. L., and Clayton, P. H. "Generating, Deepening, and Documenting Learning: The Power of Critical Reflection for Applied Learning." *Journal of Applied Learning in Higher Education*, 2009a, *1*, 25–48.

Ash, S. L., and Clayton, P. H. *Learning through Critical Reflection: A Tutorial for Students in Service-Learning (Instructor Version)*. Raleigh, N.C.: Authors, 2009b.

Ash, S. L., Clayton, P. H., and Atkinson, M. P. "Integrating Reflection and Assessment to Capture and Improve Student Learning." *Michigan Journal of Community Service Learning*, 2005, *11*, 49–60.

Astin, A. W., Vogelgesang, L. J., Ikeda, E. K., and Yee, J. A. *How Service Learning Affects Students*. Los Angeles: Higher Education Research Institute, UCLA, 2000.

Astin, A. W., and others. *Understanding the Effects of Service-Learning: A Study of Students and Faculty*. Los Angeles: Higher Education Research Institute, UCLA, 2006.

Bloom, B. S. (ed.). *Taxonomy of Educational Objectives, Handbook I: Cognitive Domain*. New York: David McKay, 1956.

Boyer, E. L. "The Scholarship of Engagement." *Journal of Public Service and Outreach*, 1996, *1*, 1.

Brandenberger, J. "Research on the Personal Development of Students in Service Learning." In P. Clayton, J. Hatcher, and R. Bringle (eds.), *Research on Service Learning: Conceptual Frameworks and Assessment* (Vol. 2). IUPUI Series on Service Learning Research. Sterling, Va.: Stylus, forthcoming.

Bringle, R., Games, R., and Malloy, E. A. "Colleges and Universities as Citizens: Reflections." In R. Bringle, R. Games, and E. A. Malloy (eds.), *Colleges and Universities as Citizens* (pp. 193–204). Needham Heights, Mass.: Allyn and Bacon, 1999.

Bringle, R., Hatcher, J., and McIntosh, R. "Analyzing Morton's Typology of Service Paradigms and Integrity." *Michigan Journal of Community Service Learning*, 2006, *13*, 5–15.

Carini, R. M., Kuh, G. D., and Klein, S. P. "Student Engagement and Student Learning: Testing the Linkages." *Research in Higher Education*, 2006, *47*, 1–32.

Clayton, P. H., and Ash, S. L. "Shifts in Perspective: Capitalizing on the Counter-Normative Nature of Service-Learning." *Michigan Journal of Community Service Learning*, 2004, *11*, 59–70.

Colby, A., and others. *Educating Citizens: Preparing America's Undergraduates for Lives of Moral and Civic Responsibility.* San Francisco: Jossey-Bass, 2003.

Cranton, P. "Fostering Authentic Relationships in the Transformative Classroom." *New Directions for Adult and Continuing Education*, 2006, *109*, 5–13.

Dewey, J. *How We Think.* Mineola, N.Y.: Dover, 1997. (Originally published 1933.)

Ehrlich, T. Foreword. In B. Jacoby and Associates, *Service-Learning in Higher Education: Concepts and Practices* (pp. xi-xvi). San Francisco: Jossey-Bass, 1996.

Eyler, J. "What International Service Learning Research Can Learn from Research on Service Learning." In R. G. Bringle, J. A. Hatcher, and S. G. Jones (eds.), *International Service Learning: Conceptual Frameworks and Research* (Vol. 2, pp. 225–242). IUPUI Series on Service Learning Research. Sterling, Va.: Stylus, 2010.

Eyler, J., and Giles, D. E., Jr. *Where's the Learning in Service-Learning?* San Francisco: Jossey-Bass, 1999.

Eyler, J. S., Giles, D. E., Jr., Stenson, C. M., and Gray, C. J. *At a Glance: What We Know about the Effects of Service-Learning on College Students, Faculty, Institutions and Communities, 1993–2000.* (3rd ed.) Nashville, Tenn.: Vanderbilt University Press, 2001.

Felten, P., Gilchrist, L. Z., and Darby, A. "Emotion and Learning: Feeling Our Way Toward a New Theory of Reflection in Service-Learning." *Michigan Journal of Community Service Learning*, 2006, *12*, 28–46.

Fitch, P. "In Their Own Voices: A Mixed-Methods Approach to Studying Intercultural Service-Learning with College Students." In S. Root, J. Callahan, and S. H. Billig (eds.), *Improving Service-Learning Practice: Research on Models to Enhance Impacts* (pp. 187–211). Greenwich, Conn.: Information Age, 2005.

Howard, J. "Academic Service Learning: A Counter Normative Pedagogy." *New Directions in Teaching and Learning*, 1998, *73*, 21–29.

Jameson, J., Clayton, P., and Ash, S. "Research on the Academic Learning of Students in Service-Learning." In P. Clayton, J. Hatcher, and R. Bringle (eds.), *Research on Service Learning: Conceptual Frameworks and Assessment* (Vol. 2). IUPUI Series on Service Learning Research. Sterling, Va.: Stylus, forthcoming.

Jameson, J., Clayton, P., and Jaeger, A. "Community Engaged Scholarship as Mutually Transformative Partnerships." In L. Harter, J. Hamel-Lambert, and J. Millesen (eds.), *Participatory Partnerships for Social Action and Research* (pp. 259–277). Dubuque, Iowa: Kendall Hunt, 2010.

Jones, S. R., and Abes, E. S. "Enduring Influences of Service-Learning on College Students' Identity Development." *Journal of College Student Development*, 2004, *45*, 149–166.

Kahne, J., and Westheimer, J. "The Limits of Political Efficacy: Educating Citizens for a Democratic Society." *PS: Political Science and Politics,* 2006, *39,* 289–296.

Kuh, G. *High-Impact Educational Practices.* Washington, D.C.: Association of American Colleges and Universities, 2008.

Lundy, B. L. "Service Learning in Life-Span Developmental Psychology: Higher Exam Scores and Increased Empathy." *Teaching of Psychology,* 2007, *34,* 23–27.

Mezirow, J., and Associates. *Learning as Transformation: Critical Perspectives on a Theory in Progress.* San Francisco: Jossey-Bass, 2000.

Mpofu, E. "Service Learning Effects on the Academic Learning of Rehabilitation Services Students." *Michigan Journal of Community Service Learning,* 2007, *14,* 46–52.

Pascarella, E. T., and Terenzini, P. T. *How College Affects Students: Vol. 2. A Third Decade of Research.* San Francisco: Jossey-Bass, 2005.

Paul, R., and Elder, L. *Critical Thinking: Tools for Taking Charge of Your Learning and Your Life.* (2nd ed.) Upper Saddle River, N.J.: Prentice Hall, 2006.

Rhoads, R. "How Civic Engagement Is Reframing Liberal Education." *Peer Review,* 2003, *5,* 25–28.

Saltmarsh, J., and Hartley, M. (eds.). *"To Serve a Larger Purpose": Engagement for Democracy and the Transformation of Higher Education.* Philadelphia: Temple University Press, 2011.

Saltmarsh, J., Hartley, M., and Clayton, P. *Democratic Engagement White Paper.* Boston: New England Resource Center for Higher Education, 2009.

Sigmon, R. "Service-Learning: Three Principles." *Synergist,* 1979, *8*(10), 9–11.

Stewart, T. "Community Collaboration for Underserved Schools: A First-Year Honors Service-Learning Seminar Approach." *Journal for Civic Commitment,* 2009, *13,* 1–16.

Strage, A. A. "Service Learning: Enhancing Student Learning Outcomes in a College-Level Lecture Course." *Michigan Journal of Community Service Learning,* 2000, *7,* 5–13.

Vandenberg, B. "Is Epistemology Enough? An Existential Consideration of Development." *American Psychologist,* 1991, *46,* 1278–1286.

Whitney, B. C., McClure, J. D., Respet, A. J., and Clayton, P. H. "Service-Learning as a Shared Developmental Journey: Tapping the Potential of the Pedagogy." In L. McIlrath and I. MacLabhrainn (eds.), *Higher Education and Civic Engagement: International Perspectives* (pp. 185–196). Burlington, Vt.: Ashgate, 2007.

Wurr, A. J. "Service Learning and Student Writing." In S. H. Billig and A. Furco (eds.), *Service Learning Through a Multidisciplinary Lens* (pp. 103–121). Greenwich, Conn.: Information Age, 2002.

PETER FELTEN *is assistant provost for teaching and learning at Elon University and president (2010–2011) of the Professional and Organizational Development Network in Higher Education.*

PATTI H. CLAYTON *is an independent consultant (PHC Ventures: www .curricularengagement.com) and a senior scholar with the Center for Service and Learning at Indiana University–Purdue University Indianapolis.*

9

This chapter describes a Web-based program based on well-researched principles of behavior. Among the innovations of the program is a peer-review component. The program has been well accepted by administrators, staff, and students at institutions where it is or has been used.

Web-Based Computer-Aided Personalized System of Instruction

Joseph J. Pear, Gabriel J. Schnerch, Kathleen M. Silva, Louis Svenningsen, Jody Lambert

In the last two decades, there has been a proliferation of Web-based course-management systems designed to facilitate postsecondary teaching (for example, WebCT, Blackboard, Desire2Learn, Moodle). In general, these systems provide analogs for delivering lectures, holding class discussions, giving quizzes and examinations (typically multiple choice), and assigning papers and group work—or some combination of these. In this chapter, we consider a Web-based program that uses empirically established principles to facilitate student learning.

Background

For over half a century, behavioral psychology has been developing a general theory applicable to numerous areas including education (Skinner, 1958, 1968). One behavioral application to education is the personalized system of instruction (PSI; Keller, 1968). Research has established that PSI is a more effective way for students to learn course material than is the traditional lecture method (Kulik, Kulik, and Bangert-Drowns, 1990; Kulik, Kulik, and Cohen, 1979). In PSI:

1. Students complete small sequential units of material at a time.
2. Students proceed at their own pace.

NEW DIRECTIONS FOR TEACHING AND LEARNING, no. 128, Winter 2011 © Wiley Periodicals, Inc.
Published online in Wiley Online Library (wileyonlinelibrary.com) • DOI: 10.1002/tl.471

3. Students must demonstrate mastery of a given unit before proceeding to the next unit.
4. Correct responses are immediately reinforced.
5. Aversive control is minimized. (Rather than receiving a "fail" on a unit test that is not passed, students receive a "restudy," which permits them to take a new test on the unit.)

Traditional PSI utilizes students (proctors) from a more advanced course to grade and provide feedback to students on their assignments (unit tests).

The first author (Pear) of this chapter began using traditional PSI in 1968. A major problem that he noted was the large amount of work and time necessary to run the system, which detracted from the amount of time he could interact with students. Pear collaborated with Witold Kinsner, a professor of electrical and computer engineering at the University of Manitoba, to produce a computer-aided personalized system of instruction (CAPSI; Kinsner and Pear, 1988; Pear and Kinsner, 1988) that operated on the university's mainframe computer. One advantage of computerizing PSI was that it reduced the need to utilize proctors external to the course. Because computers can access information about the level of mastery of any student at any time, when a unit test is submitted, the computer can select students who have already mastered that particular unit in the course to be proctors. In traditional PSI, and in CAPSI prior to 2004, students from within a course who serve as proctors are called internal proctors (Sherman, 1977). Since the advent of WebCAPSI (a Web-based version of CAPSI), students who provide feedback to other students within Web-CAPSI courses are called peer reviewers.

In 1994, the CAPSI program was rewritten in DOS and became accessible on personal computers. Students could access the program from anywhere (Pear and Crone-Todd, 1999). In 1996, Pear proposed that in place of each course he would normally be assigned, he would teach four distinct undergraduate courses, provided that he did not have to have regularly scheduled class meetings. The department head agreed to this arrangement. This teaching load was feasible because once the material for each CAPSI course was prepared, it was not appreciably more difficult to teach several courses than it was to teach just one course. The main determinant of workload for CAPSI teachers when no classroom or regular meeting times are scheduled is not the number of courses they are teaching but the total enrollment of students within those courses. However, workload does not increase proportionately with total enrollment because the number of peer reviewers also increases.

CAPSI can also be used with regularly scheduled classes. Students learn the basic concepts through CAPSI while regular meeting times are reserved for lectures, student presentations, and class discussions.

In 2004, because of the clear benefits of CAPSI (described later in this chapter), the University of Manitoba funded the development of a

Web-based version of the program, WebCAPSI. (Note: "CAPSI" refers to the general method while "WebCAPSI" refers to the current program for instantiating CAPSI on the Web.) Students and instructors can access WebCAPSI using computers or handheld devices that can connect to the Internet (for example, BlackBerry, iPhone).

CAPSI's Psychological and Educational Underpinnings and Connections

Dividing course material into small units is consistent with the idea that learning is more effective if it proceeds gradually. Providing students with study questions fits with the behavioral approach of clearly defining the behavior to be learned. Providing rapid feedback is consistent with the behavioral principle that immediate reinforcement is more effective than delayed reinforcement in strengthening and maintaining behavior. Requiring answers to be in essay format is consistent with the view that effective writing is an important skill that is best developed through practice. (For detailed information on setting up a CAPSI course, visit www.CAPSI.org.)

A common criticism of many postsecondary courses is that students often are not taught to engage in critical or higher-level thinking. Because CAPSI deals in questions and answers, critical-thinking skills can be defined on the basis of Bloom's taxonomy (Bloom and others, 1956; Crone-Todd and Pear, 2001; Crone-Todd, Pear, and Read, 2000; Pear, 2002; Pear, Crone-Todd, Wirth, and Simister, 2001; Pear and Martin, 2004). Through the use of Bloom's taxonomy, one can ensure that sufficient higher-level questions are provided in a CAPSI course. For detailed descriptions of this use of Bloom's taxonomy, see Crone-Todd, Pear, and Read (2000) and Pear and others (2001).

There are two other ways in which CAPSI develops higher-order thinking: peer reviewing and appeals. Students judge whether another student's answers meet specific mastery criteria, which frequently requires peer reviewers to make judgments at a higher level than the questions being asked. CAPSI also contains a built-in appeal process (similar to that used in team-based learning; see the article by Michaelsen and Sweet in this volume). Students can present arguments as to why their answers meet mastery criteria after receiving feedback from peer reviewers that their answers did not meet mastery criteria. Their arguments often require a higher level of thinking than the original questions did.

CAPSI is consistent with social constructivism (that is, the construction of knowledge through social interaction) (Pear and Crone-Todd, 2002). Through mutual reinforcement and feedback, under the guidance of the instructor, students gradually develop a deep understanding of the key concepts of the subject matter.

CAPSI emphasizes both formative and summative evaluation (Bloom, Hastings, and Madaus, 1971). Formative assessment occurs through writing answers to unit questions and through peer reviewing unit tests. Summative evaluation occurs through assessing students' knowledge via examinations that are also provided via WebCAPSI.

Benefits

CAPSI results in benefits to the department and university, to teachers, and the students. Although we discuss each of these categories separately, there are large overlaps among them. Some of the benefits described are also applicable to other computerized instructional systems, but it is not clear that these other systems use empirically established principles.

Benefits to the Department and University. When used without regularly scheduled class meetings, CAPSI allows a greater variety of courses to be offered. It also allows more students to take more courses without adding to administrative or building costs because much of the course work is done from other locations, thereby freeing classroom space for other purposes. In addition, there are fewer schedule conflicts, including conflicts with jobs and other responsibilities that students may have apart from their course work.

Because CAPSI can be used as part of regularly scheduled classes, departments provide a richer educational experience by encompassing a variety of different approaches to teaching as opposed to only a few. Moreover, to the extent that "consumer satisfaction" (see the "Benefits to Students" section) is correlated with higher rates of student retention (DeShields, Kara, and Kaynak, 2005) and fundraising (Elliott and Shin, 2002); the use of CAPSI may positively affect a university's budget.

Benefits to Teachers. When used as an alternative to delivering course content by lecturing, CAPSI allows teachers to devote more time to other pedagogical activities. For example, teachers can spend more time discussing academic material with students individually or in groups, helping students with research, and preparing academic materials for students. In Pear's case, much of the academic material prepared for his CAPSI courses evolved into books (for example, Martin and Pear, 2011; Pear, 2001, 2007).

In some cases, CAPSI has been used to teach a particular component of a course rather than the entire course. Teachers lecture or hold discussion groups during some portion of a course while covering other portions using CAPSI. This method is particularly useful for those components where the content is more structured, such as learning the *Publication Manual of the American Psychological Association* (APA style) in a research methods course. Other topics, such as critical thinking, have been successfully taught by tying the presentation of in-class material to practice and mastery of basic components (critical assessment and writing) using CAPSI. Thus, hybrid courses using CAPSI have effectively married in-class and virtual instruction. As a window on the educational process, CAPSI also provides

NEW DIRECTIONS FOR TEACHING AND LEARNING • DOI: 10.1002/tl

a means of conducting educational research, which is facilitated by Web-CAPSI's capability to archive all data generated by the program.

Benefits to Students. Students rate CAPSI courses high in "consumer satisfaction" (for example, Pear and Novak, 1996). They particularly like the time convenience, the flexibility it provides for their schedules, and the straightforward expectations of the method. In addition, a majority of students indicate that they learn as much in CAPSI courses as they did in more traditionally taught courses. When CAPSI is used with regularly scheduled class meetings and lecturing, students commonly remark that they could not have learned the subject matter so well without the use of CAPSI.

CAPSI Research Studies

CAPSI has been used at the University of Manitoba for almost thirty years. Research into it has been going on for almost as long. Next we summarize some of what this research has shown.

Operating Characteristics. At the beginning of a course, the teacher or teaching assistants do a considerable amount of reviewing (that is, giving feedback on unit tests). Toward the end of the course, students are doing almost all of the reviewing (Kinsner and Pear, 1990; Pear and Crone-Todd, 2002; Pear and Martin, 2004), which leaves the teacher with time to oversee test writing, to provide feedback on student reviews, to answer appeals, and to deal with other parts of the course (for example, exams, papers, lectures, and discussion groups).

Comparisons with Other Teaching Methods. Svenningsen (2009), in two introductions to the university courses, compared CAPSI with an extra paper assignment, and in an introduction to psychology course he compared CAPSI to weekly multiple-choice quizzes. He found that student performance on various measures (for example, examination scores) was higher in the CAPSI sections than in the non-CAPSI sections. Although these results did not always reach statistical significance, the fact that they were always in the direction favoring CAPSI attests to the viability of the method.

CAPSI has also been proven to be effective in teaching APA style in a psychological research methods course taught by one of the authors (Silva). After CAPSI was introduced into the course, students scored about 10 to 15 percent higher on a practical, in-class examination to assess their knowledge of APA style. In addition, students' major research papers improved in terms of clarity, content, and APA style.

Correlates of Success in a CAPSI Course. Pear and Novak (1996) found that the greatest predictor of success in a CAPSI course, where "success" was defined as performance on a heavily weighted final exam, is prior grade-point average (GPA). When prior GPA is disregarded, there are moderate correlations among how rapidly students progress through the course,

NEW DIRECTIONS FOR TEACHING AND LEARNING • DOI: 10.1002/tl

the amount of peer reviewing they do, and their final examination performance (Springer and Pear, 2008). Springer and Pear also found that students who complete all unit tests regardless of when they start or how fast they complete the units obtain higher final exam scores than students who do not complete all units. Moreover, Silva (unpublished course data, 2011) has noted that the correlation between the number of unit tests completed and scores on related exams and assignments can be quite high (e.g., $r = .60$ to .80).

Higher-Order Thinking. Crone-Todd (2002) demonstrated that when extra reinforcement (for example, bonus points, praise) is provided for higher-order thinking on CAPSI unit tests and examinations, students answered questions at higher thinking levels than they did when this extra reinforcement was not provided. Thus, thinking levels can be increased by positive reinforcement using CAPSI.

Accuracy and Quality of Peer Feedback. Accuracy of student feedback is almost as high as feedback from the instructor or teaching assistants (Martin, Pear, and Martin, 2002a), which is due largely to the fact that (at least when the course is well designed) the majority of unit tests completed by students reach criterion level for a "pass" grade. Peer reviewers tend to be more reluctant than teachers or teaching assistants to assign restudies. However, peer reviewers often still give good feedback on problems in a student's answer even when giving a pass rather than a restudy (Martin, Pear, and Martin, 2002a).

Based on some of Martin, Pear, and Martin's (2002b) recommendations for types of peer-reviewer feedback that would be most effective, Schnerch, Devine, and Pear (2007) developed a *Peer-Reviewer Training Manual (PRTM)* for CAPSI. Boehr and others (2008) found that, when measured against a comparison group, students provided with *PRTM* training gave substantially more corrective and positive feedback.

Procrastination. One of the features that students indicated that they like about CAPSI is that it allows them to proceed through the course at their own pace. Although self-pacing can give rise to procrastination, it appears that students who procrastinate do just as well on the final exam as students who complete the work earlier—provided that those students who procrastinate finish all the units before the end of the course (Springer and Pear, 2008). Adding deadlines to a course may, however, tend to increase dropout rate (Schnerch, 2007). Thus, procrastination is not a problem if students give themselves enough time to complete the units before the end of the course.

Peer Reviewing. GPA explains most of the variance in both peer reviewing points and final exam scores (Pear and Novak, 1996). Springer and Pear (2008) found little effect of peer reviewing on final exam performance once rate of progress through the course was partitioned out. Lambert (2009) also found no difference on the final exam between a section in which there were peer reviewers and a section in which the grading of unit tests was done entirely by the teacher and teaching assistants.

Although peer reviewing has not been empirically shown to enhance final exam performance, on course questionnaires given in CAPSI courses, students overwhelmingly indicate that serving as peer reviewers helped them learn the course material. The perception of a beneficial effect may occur because students are able to answer higher-level questions with greater ease or have a greater retention of course content as a result of peer reviewing.

Future Research. A commitment to empirical research is critical to the continued development of CAPSI. Future studies could investigate four variables in particular.

1. *The optimal number of points to award for unit test completion.* Given that completing unit tests is positively correlated with performance on other assessments, it is desirable that students complete all units and do so without procrastinating. Manipulating the number of points earned for completing a unit test is one option. For example, making later units worth more points than earlier units may motivate students to start their units earlier so they complete all units by the deadline.

2. *The optimal number of points to award for peer reviewing.* Because students perceive peer reviewing as beneficial to their learning, and because it appears to promote higher-level thinking and greater retention of course content, it is desirable for students to serve as peer reviewers. What is unknown is how many points should be awarded for peer reviewing and whether this number depends on other factors, such as how many points are awarded for mastering a unit.

3. *The optimal number of peer reviewers per unit test.* Two peer reviewers inject a degree of quality control into the system; with two peer reviewers, students receive more accurate feedback, and more tests that should receive a "restudy" recommendation actually receive them (Martin, Pear, and Martin, 2002b). The question, then, is whether and to what extent more peer reviewers per unit test would provide even more quality control.

4. *The most effective quantity and frequency of feedback that a teacher or teaching assistant should provide to peer reviewers to increase the quality of their feedback.* Should peer reviewers be awarded points commensurate with the quality of their feedback, and what proportion of peer reviewers' feedback should be rewarded?

Conclusion

Overall, CAPSI has been well accepted as an alternative to traditional teaching methods and to other forms of Web-based instruction. More important, it embodies sound pedagogical principles based on empirical research, and it provides a tool for conducting research on the educational process.

References

Bloom, B. S., and others. *Taxonomy of Educational Objectives*. New York: Longmans, Green, 1956.

Bloom, B. S., Hastings, T., and Madaus, G. *Handbook of Formative and Summative Evaluation of Student Learning*. New York: McGraw-Hill, 1971.

Boehr, B. J., and others. "Effects of a Peer-Reviewer Training Manual on Quality of Peer-Reviewer Feedback in a Computer-Aided Personalized System of Instruction Course." Poster presented at the 34th Annual Convention of the Association for Behavior Analysis, Chicago, Illinois, May 2008.

Crone-Todd, D. E. "Increasing the Levels at which Undergraduate Students Answer Questions in a Computer-Aided Personalized System of Instruction Course." Unpublished Ph.D. dissertation, University of Manitoba, Winnipeg, Manitoba, 2002.

Crone-Todd, D. E., and Pear, J. J. "Application of Bloom's Taxonomy to PSI." *Behavior Analyst Today*, 2001, *3*, 204–210.

Crone-Todd, D. E., Pear, J. J., and Read, C. N. "Operational Definitions for Higher-Order Thinking Objectives at the Post-Secondary Level." *Academic Exchange Quarterly*, 2000, *4*(3), 99–106.

DeShields, O. W., Jr., Kara, A., and Kaynak, E. "Determinants of Business Student Satisfaction and Retention in Higher Education: Applying Herzberg's Two-Factor Theory." *International Journal of Educational Management*, 2005, *19*, 128–139.

Elliott, K. M., and Shin, D. "Student Satisfaction: An Alternative Approach to Assessing This Important Concept." *Journal of Higher Education Policy and Management*, 2002, *24*, 197–209.

Keller, F. S. "Good-bye Teacher . . ." *Journal of Applied Behavior Analysis*, 1968, *1*, 79–89.

Kinsner, W., and Pear, J. J. "Computer-Aided Personalized System of Instruction for the Virtual Classroom." *Canadian Journal of Educational Communication*, 1988, *17*, 21–36.

Kinsner, W., and Pear, J. J. "Dynamic Educational System for the Virtual Campus." In U. E. Gattiker (ed.), *Studies in Technological Innovation and Human Resources. Vol. 2: End-User Training* (pp. 201–228). Berlin: Walter de Gruyter, 1990.

Kulik, C.-L., Kulik, J. A., and Bangert-Drowns, R. L. "Effectiveness of Mastery Learning Programs: A Meta-Analysis." *Review of Educational Research*, 1990, *60*, 265–299.

Kulik, J. A., Kulik, C.-L., and Cohen, P. "A Meta-Analysis of Outcome Studies of Keller's Personalized System of Instruction." *American Psychologist*, 1979, *34*, 307–318.

Lambert, J. "Effects of the Peer-Reviewer Component of a Computer-Aided PSI Course." Unpublished M.A. thesis, University of Manitoba, Winnipeg, Manitoba, 2009.

Martin, G., and Pear, J. *Behavior Modification: What It Is and How to Do It*. (9th ed.) Upper Saddle River, N.J.: Pearson Prentice Hall, 2011.

Martin, T. L., Pear, J. J., and Martin, G. L. "Analysis of Proctor Marking Accuracy in a Computer-Aided Personalized System of Instruction Course." *Journal of Applied Behavior Analysis*, 2002a, *35*, 309–312.

Martin, T. L., Pear, J. J., and Martin, G. L. "Feedback and Its Effectiveness in a Computer-Aided Personalized System of Instruction Course." *Journal of Applied Behavior Analysis*, 2002b, *35*, 427–430.

Michaelsen, L. K., and Sweet, M. "Team-Based Learning." In W. Buskist and J. E. Groccia (eds.), *Evidence-Based Teaching*. New Directions for Teaching and Learning. San Francisco: Jossey-Bass, 2011, *128*.

Pear, J. J. *The Science of Learning*. Philadelphia: Psychology Press, 2001.

Pear, J. J. "Teaching and Researching Higher-Order Thinking in a Virtual Environment." In J. A. Chambers (ed.), *Selected Papers from the 13th International Conference on College Teaching and Learning* (pp. 143–150). Jacksonville: Florida Community College at Jacksonville, 2002.

Pear, J. J. "A Historical and Contemporary Look at Psychological Systems." Mahwah, N.J.: Lawrence Erlbaum, 2007.

Pear, J. J., and Crone-Todd, D. E. "Personalized System of Instruction in Cyberspace." *Journal of Applied Behavior Analysis*, 1999, *32*, 205–209.

Pear, J. J., and Crone-Todd, D. E. "A Social Constructivist Approach to Computer-Mediated Instruction." *Computers and Education*, 2002, *38*, 221–231.

Pear, J. J., Crone-Todd, D. E., Wirth, K., and Simister, H. "Assessment of Thinking Levels in Students' Answers." *Academic Exchange Quarterly*, 2001, *5*(4), 94–98.

Pear, J. J., and Kinsner, W. "Computer-Aided Personalized System of Instruction: An Effective and Economical Method for Short- and Long-Distance Education." *Machine-Mediated Learning*, 1988, *2*, 213–237.

Pear, J. J., and Martin, T. L. "Making the Most of PSI with Computer Technology." In D. J. Moran and R. W. Malott (eds.), *Evidence-Based Educational Methods* (pp. 223–243). San Diego: Elsevier and Academic Press, 2004.

Pear, J. J., and Novak, M. "Computer-Aided Personalized System of Instruction: A Program Evaluation." *Teaching of Psychology*, 1996, *23*, 119–123.

Schnerch, G. J. "A Study of Procrastination in a Computer-Aided Personalized System of Instruction Course." Unpublished M.A. thesis, University of Manitoba, Winnipeg, Manitoba, 2007.

Schnerch, G. J., Devine, S., and Pear, J. J. *Peer-Reviewer Training Manual for Computer-Aided Personalized System of Instruction (CAPSI)*. Winnipeg, Canada: University of Manitoba Bookstore, 2007.

Sherman, J. G. "Individualizing Instruction Is Not Enough." *Educational Technology*, 1977, *17*, 56–60.

Silva, K. M. Correlations between units completed and grades on exams and other assignments in WebCAPSI courses. Unpublished paper, Department of Psychology, University of Redlands, Redlands, California, United States, 2011.

Skinner, B. F. "Teaching Machines." *Science*, 1958, *129*, 969–977.

Skinner, B. F. *The Technology of Teaching*. New York: Appleton-Century-Crofts, 1968.

Springer, C. R., and Pear, J. J. "Performance Measures in Courses Using Computer-Aided Personalized System of Instruction." *Computers and Education*, 2008, *51*, 829–835.

Svenningsen, L. "An Examination of the Effect of CAPSI as a Learning System in Developing Knowledge and Critical Thinking in Two Blended Learning Courses." Unpublished Ph.D. dissertation, University of Manitoba, Winnipeg, Manitoba, 2009.

JOSEPH J. PEAR *is a professor of psychology at the University of Manitoba. He developed CAPSI, conducts and supervises research on CAPSI, and uses it in all his courses.*

GABRIEL J. SCHNERCH *is a board-certified behavior analyst and a student in the Ph.D. program in clinical psychology at the University of Manitoba.*

KATHLEEN M. SILVA *is an associate professor of psychology at the University of Redlands.*

LOUIS SVENNINGSEN *is an instruction technologist in the Centre for Teaching, Learning, and Technology at the University of Winnipeg.*

JODY LAMBERT *is a behavior analyst in the Community Support Program at St. Amant and a master's student in the Marriage and Family Therapy program at the University of Winnipeg.*

10

This chapter provides a brief history of online learning and a discussion of the empirical evidence for its acceptance and effectiveness.

Online Learning

Edward H. Perry, Michelle L. Pilati

Although the Internet had its beginnings in 1969 as a creation of the Department of Defense, it did not become a driving force in the world until twenty years later, when Tim Berners-Lee of the European Organization for Nuclear Research conceived of what we now know as the World Wide Web. Berners-Lee and a colleague introduced the Web to the rest of the world in August 1991, and two years later, when a group at the University of Illinois launched Mosaic, the first graphical Web browser, "the Web" became a household term.

Distance education, which began as correspondence courses in the nineteenth century and grew into educational television during the twentieth century, evolved into learning on the Web by the mid-1990s. In 2002, over 1.6 million postsecondary students were enrolled in online courses, and six years later, this number had almost tripled (Allen and Seaman, 2010). Over 25 percent of all higher education students in 2008 were taking at least one online class, and online enrollments numbers were growing by 17 percent annually compared with 1.2 percent for higher education as a whole (Allen and Seaman, 2010). As the first decade of the new century drew to a close, online learning had become a major element in the higher education matrix. The mail-delivered correspondence course of yesterday had become the Web-delivered online course of today.

Accompanying the rise in online learning has been a similar rise in organizations and publications dedicated to serving the needs of online educators and exploring issues related to this evolving instructional modality. Sloan-C (Sloan Consortium; www.sloanconsortium.org), MERLOT (Multimedia Resource for Learning and Online Teaching; www.merlot.org)

NEW DIRECTIONS FOR TEACHING AND LEARNING, no. 128, Winter 2011 © Wiley Periodicals, Inc.
Published online in Wiley Online Library (wileyonlinelibrary.com) • DOI: 10.1002/tl.472

and NSDL (National Science Digital Library; www.nsdl.org) are but three of the many organizations that have emerged in the last decade to provide online resources for both classroom instructors and their online counterparts.

On its homepage, Sloan-C describes itself as "an institutional and professional leadership organization dedicated to integrating online education into the mainstream of higher education." It is a member-supported, nonprofit group that hosts several annual conferences and provides publications of interest to the online teaching community.

MERLOT currently provides links to over 20,000 online teaching materials along with peer reviews for many of these. An open-access organization with no individual membership fees, MERLOT is supported by institutional partners across the country and has branches in Africa and South America. In 2005, MERLOT added an online peer-reviewed journal, the *Journal of Online Learning and Teaching* (*JOLT*), which publishes scholarly manuscripts related specifically to online learning and teaching.

According to its Web site, NSDL is "the Nation's online library for education and research in Science, Technology, Engineering, and Mathematics." It provides links to dozens of collections that share information about their individual resources.

There are also many scholarly journals devoted to distance education in general and online education in particular. In addition to *JOLT*, these include:

American Journal of Distance Education (www.ajde.com)
Journal of Asynchronous Learning Networks (www.sloanconsortium.org
    /publications/jaln_main)
Journal of Distance Education (www.jofde.ca/index.php/jde)
Journal of Interactive Online Learning (www.ncolr.org/jiol/)
Journal of Educators Online (www.thejeo.com)
Online Journal of Distance Learning Administration (www.westga
    .edu/~distance/ojdla/)

Thus, online learning has become entrenched in the educational scene. It is only expected to grow during the coming years as more students demand it and as more faculty accept it. Despite the growth of online instruction and the unique needs it addresses, it has not achieved universal acceptance, and there are those who hold distance education to higher standards than traditional instruction. Any institution or teacher seeking to venture into the online realm needs to be fully aware of these emerging challenges. The prospect of greater scrutiny, however, may prompt the development of online offerings that exceed traditional quality and effectiveness expectations.

NEW DIRECTIONS FOR TEACHING AND LEARNING • DOI: 10.1002/tl

Online Learning and Its Implementation

Online teaching exists in many forms. This modern form of distance education offers a wide array of features that were never possible with correspondence courses and instructional television. "Correspondence" is now achieved with a number of tools that permit synchronous and asynchronous communication and collaboration. Online instructors are aided by robust tools that provide assessments and ever-increasing options for the delivery of course content. Today there is much exploration of how to implement online instruction most effectively, which often includes a combination of "traditional" face-to-face instruction and online instruction. A review of the literature relating to distance education from the early 1980s reveals an understandable lack of knowledge of the role that technology would play today in our lives and of the opportunities for advancing all forms of education that technology now provides.

There are no exacting definitions in the online realm—one college's online course may be another's hybrid, and one college's hybrid course may be another's blended or Web-enhanced course. What is critical at the system or institutional level is that the nature of the course is communicated effectively to students. Although access to the Internet may appear to be ubiquitous, a digital divide—some students are Internet savvy and some are not—still exists (Kleinman, 2001), and students must be aware of Internet access requirements in advance of course selection. Some institutions address this matter by establishing policies with respect to such access (for example, explicitly stating that all students are expected to have and use Internet access for all classes) whereas others with more diverse populations may prohibit such policies because they would further disadvantage students who do not have regular and/or reliable access to the Internet.

Within the public sector, online instruction has been most fully accepted by community colleges that seek to provide educational opportunities for an extremely diverse student population, requiring sensitivity to issues of differential connectivity. But even within segments of higher education that can assume ready access and relative online proficiency, it still must be recognized that online instruction is not for every student, nor for every faculty member. In addition, some disciplines are less well suited to online teaching. Great debate continues to exist as to whether science lab courses can be offered effectively online, and many teachers question the appropriateness of public speaking courses taught online, just to note a couple of areas where online instruction has not been fully embraced (Abdel-Salam, Kauffmann, and Crossman, 2007).

"Hybrid" or "blended" instruction involves a combination of online and in-classroom instruction. The nature of such courses can vary widely. Some courses are taught in a compressed format, where the online component permits the course to progress at twice its normal pace by offering a traditional-length lecture over half the term. Other courses may involve course elements that require face-to-face contact and meet just a few times during the term, such as a course that requires in-person presentations. The options are truly unlimited, and exploration in this realm is active and ongoing.

What is clear is that the factors that enhance the educational experience in a classroom—community, timely feedback, clear expectations, and a reasonable chance of success—are equally important for online learning (Chickering and Ehrmann, 1996; Sadera, Robertson, Song, and Midon, 2009). If such fundamentals are ignored when a course is delivered either partially or fully online, student success will be negatively impacted. Merely understanding the technology involved in online delivery will not suffice, and merely re-creating the classroom in the online realm does not produce a satisfying or effective experience. Creating a learning environment that fosters success requires appropriate use of both pedagogy and technology (Menchaca and Bekele, 2008).

In the United States, higher education is facing new challenges as it seeks to welcome nontraditional students and nontraditional forms of instruction while maintaining quality and addressing increasing calls for accountability (WICHE Cooperative for Technical Education [WCET], 2008). New online instructors need to be prepared to answer the seemingly simple question: How do you know who is taking your course? Developing a course with this question in mind will lead to a better course and a better student experience. Online instructors should be mindful of the need to "know" their students through the use of a variety of forms of interaction throughout the duration of the course. Just as face-to-face instructors know their students by sight, online instructors should come to know their students through the quality of their work, their writing, and their online presence. One-on-one communications, written assignments, and discussion postings all provide instructors with samples of student skills and abilities. The opportunities for such interactions should be continuous and well integrated. The thinking, skill level, writing style, and personal views exhibited by students in an online discussion should be consistent with those demonstrated in a written assignment or a personal communication. Online instructors should monitor student contributions for consistency and regularly initiate a variety of interactions with students as one means of ensuring course integrity. Attention to such opportunities for interaction can serve to better engage the student and aid in the creation of an effective online community (Vesely, Bloom, and Sherlock, 2007).

Online instruction provides faculty with a chance to be more purposeful in their teaching and to offer students more opportunities to interact with course materials. It removes the confines of the clock and the classroom, which may improve or diminish outcomes. It is critical that the expectations faculty have of student performance neither increase nor decrease in the online environment. Equally critical is that time on task remains the same for students. Online instruction should provide students who need additional time to absorb material to do so and allow students who can move more quickly to do so, within reason. Student–student interaction is often lacking in an online course—but need not be. Just as community and belonging are important in face-to-face instruction, so they are in online instruction. Thus, all students must progress through some course components at the same pace, such as a course-related discussion forum.

An additional consideration when developing online offerings is accessibility. Courses need to be developed with the various needs or limitations of end users in mind. Just as such accommodations can positively impact students in the traditional classroom, there are even more such opportunities in the online realm. An "alt tag," for example, that provides a description of an image for the blind student may also offer an explanation of why the image is significant, providing useful information to all students. Integrating such accommodations will also serve the various types of learners present in all classes.

Concerns about the quality of online instruction are real and well publicized. Academic integrity must be integrated into online offerings—not an afterthought. Without a purposeful approach to addressing the concerns of those who would seek to mandate proctored in-person student assessment, the promise of online instruction will not be realized and will be tainted by concerns regarding its legitimacy (Baron and Crooks, 2005).

Review of the Empirical Evidence

Distance education has always appealed to students who live far from learning centers or who have limitations that make in-person attendance challenging or impossible, and online learning is no exception. It offers learning anytime anywhere and fits well into modern lifestyles where the Internet is seemingly ever present. Online learning also appeals to university administrators because of its potential cost effectiveness and its ability to bring about learning in a global classroom. It must be kept in mind, though, that while online instruction may not always be more cost effective, it does permit online courses to be expanded without the limitation of classroom availability.

At least three issues arise when the effectiveness of online education is examined. First is the student perception of online learning. Do students feel they receive as good an education online as they would in a face-to-face classroom? Second is that of faculty perceptions. Are faculty members who are accustomed to face-to-face teaching in the classroom willing to adopt the new paradigm of online teaching? Finally and foremost is whether educational outcomes show online learning to be as effective as learning in traditional classrooms.

Student Perceptions. Students take online courses for a variety of reasons, including convenience and availability. Flexibility and less need to be on campus are two features most appealing to students considering online learning (Rodriguez, Ooms, and Montañez, 2008). Because most online courses are taught asynchronously, students can access course materials at times and places convenient to them. In addition, students are not limited to course offerings at a local campus; they may enroll in online courses across the country or around the world. Online offerings permit students with work or family obligations to reach their educational goals more quickly, even maintaining full-time status while significantly engaged in other endeavors.

Student perceptions of online learning are generally positive with most students reporting a moderate to high level of satisfaction with their online learning experience (Rodriguez, Ooms, and Montañez, 2008; Somenarain, Akkaraju, and Gharbaran, 2010). Although research with respect to interactivity and social presence in the online realm is mixed, it is clear that efforts toward promoting such components are worthwhile for faculty members who seek to replicate the positive components of the classroom experience that can be lacking in the online realm (for example, Dow, 2008; McInnerney and Roberts, 2004; Richardson and Swan, 2003).

Online learning requires students to be more self-motivated than traditional students who physically face their instructors and colleagues on a regular basis. Online students are much more on their own to learn the material. As a result, attrition rates are often 10 to 20 percent higher in online classes (Angelino, Williams, and Natvig, 2007). Song, Singleton, Hill, and Koh (2004) found that 71 percent of the students who were less satisfied with online learning than traditional learning cited a lack of community as a major element in their dissatisfaction. Given the dramatic increase of technology as a means of social connection, however, we may see a time when establishing community in an online class occurs as readily as it does in the classroom (Hoffman, 2009).

Rodriguez, Ooms, and Montañez (2008) found that among students who had experience with online courses, 49 percent least liked the limited face-to-face contact in online courses. This number increased to nearly 68 percent among students who had no online course experience or who had taken at least one hybrid online course. Although faculty may view hybrid offerings as the best of both worlds, students may view a course with both online and classroom commitments as the worst of both. Research examining classroom students' responses to the incorporation of online modules indicates the need to make such changes with much planning and sensitivity to the development of effective and engaging online add-ons (Smart and Cappel, 2006).

Faculty Perceptions. One of the major barriers to online learning is finding faculty members willing to learn a new way of teaching. According to Allen and Seaman (2010), fewer than one-third of chief academic officers surveyed believe their faculty accept the value and legitimacy of online education, and this fraction actually has fallen in the past two years. It is highest (44 percent) among academic officers at two-year institutions and lowest (11 percent) among those at baccalaureate colleges. Unfortunately, there are faculty members who opt to teach online but do not invest time in, or are not provided with, the pedagogical and technological training necessary to maximize the online experience for both teachers and students.

Online teaching is not simply a matter of posting lecture notes on the Web. Much more thought than that must go into the design of a Web-based course. In addition to learning new technology, faculty members moving into the online environment must also learn best practices for online learning, and many are unsure that the effort they spend in developing online courses will be reflected in tenure and promotion decisions (Brown, 2009). Faculty concerns also include the perception that online learning simply does not accomplish the same or better outcomes than traditional learning, that online learning is more susceptible to fraud, and that studies that show online learning outcomes are comparable to those found in traditional courses should be taken with a good measure of skepticism (Peabody, 2001).

Stewart, Bachman, and Johnson (2010) found that nearly 70 percent of faculty members surveyed felt online degrees are not so prestigious as those earned in face-to-face settings, and almost 50 percent felt students receiving online degrees would not have the same workforce opportunities as students who complete traditional degrees. Such perceptions are major impediments to the expansion of online learning.

Evidence of Effectiveness. Although many studies have been reported over the past ten to fifteen years on the effectiveness of online learning, by far the most comprehensive is that conducted by the U.S. Department of Education (Means and others, 2010) that examined over 1,000 empirical studies of online learning reported in the literature from 1996 through 2008. Although the study reached a number of conclusions, the most pertinent are listed next.

- Students who took all or part of their class online performed better, on average, than those taking the same course through traditional face-to-face instruction.
- Instruction combining online and face-to-face elements had a larger advantage relative to purely face-to-face instruction, which had a larger advantage relative to purely online instruction, where "advantage" refers to the learning effectiveness of the various instructional approaches (that is, hybrid online instruction was more effective than purely online).
- The effectiveness of online learning approaches appears quite broad across different content and learner types. The effectiveness of online learning was similar for undergraduates, graduate students, and professionals and was independent of the subject being learned.

However, the report also noted that differences existed between the online and classroom conditions with respect to time on task, the curriculum, and pedagogy employed. The combination of these differences might have led to additional learning time and additional opportunities for collaboration, which in turn led to the better outcomes observed. Nonetheless, this analysis makes a strong case that online learning is as effective as traditional learning.

Conclusions

Online learning, the latest manifestation of distance education, has had a major impact on higher education in the past fifteen years with over 25 percent of today's students taking online courses. It offers the flexibility desired by today's students and the cost effectiveness desired by today's college administrators. Research has shown that online learning can be just as effective, if not more so, than classroom-based learning. Efforts must be made to provide the online learner with a sense of community and to overcome the lack of face-to-face encounters with an instructor. However, faculty members must be convinced that online learning is indeed effective and that time spent in developing online learning approaches is well spent and will be rewarded.

A challenge with any new and must-do initiative is the hasty manner in which such endeavors may be adopted. Quality online teaching and learning does not occur naturally. Faculty members need training and support in the development of online materials, and both faculty members and students need support during the delivery of online classes. The lack of support for online teaching should be viewed as the equivalent of providing traditional faculty members with poorly equipped classrooms. Although some may view distance education as a cost-effective means of expanding course offerings, this perspective is shortsighted and unrealistic. Quality online instruction may be more costly than classroom instruction, but it has the benefit of providing instruction without geographical or physical barriers. Online students must have access to the same resources as traditional students. Efforts to provide online students with access to all forms of student services could benefit traditional students as well because some efficiencies may be achieved by serving both groups with technology-based support systems. Online instruction will never be the only teaching modality available—nor should it be. Teachers who venture into the online realm should do so with a clear understanding that although teaching online may be easy, doing it well is not.

References

Abdel-Salam, T. M., Kauffmann, P. J., and Crossman, G. R. "Are Distance Laboratories Effective Tools for Technology Education?" *American Journal of Distance Education,* 2007, 21, 77–91.

Allen, I. E., and Seaman, J. "Learning on Demand: Online Education in the United States, 2009. Research Report No. 7, 2010. http://www.sloan-c.org/publications/survey/pdf/learningondemand.pdf

Angelino, L., Williams, F., and Natvig, D. "Strategies to Engage Online Students and Reduce Attrition Rates." *Journal of Educators Online*, 2007, *4*. http://www.thejeo.com /Volume4Number2/Angelino%20Final.pdf

Baron, J., and Crooks, S. M. "Academic Integrity in Web-Based Distance Education." *TechTrends*, 2005, *49*(2), 40–45.

Brown, M. "Faculty Perceptions of Online Learning," 2009. http://www.ehow.com /about_5333478_faculty-perceptions-online-learning.html

Chickering, A. W., and Ehrmann, S. C. "Implementing the Seven Principles: Technology as Lever." *American Association for Higher Education Bulletin*, Oct. 1996, 3–6. http://www.tltgroup.org/programs/seven.html

Dow, M. "Implications of Social Presence for Online Learning: A Case Study of MLS Students." *Journal of Education for Library and Information Science*, 2008, *49*, 231–242.

Hoffman, E. S. "Evaluating Social Networking Tools for Distance Learning." *Proceedings of the 2009 Technology, Colleges, and Community (TCC) Conference*. http://etec.hawaii.edu/proceedings/2009/hoffman.pdf

Kleinman, S. "Understanding the Digital Divide: Implications for College Teaching." *Transformations*, 2001, *12*(2), 51–67,108.

McInnerney, J. M., and Roberts, T. S. "Online Learning: Social Interaction and the Creation of a Sense of Community." *Educational Technology and Society*, 2004, *7*, 73–81.

Means, B., and others. "Evaluation of Evidence-Based Practices in Online Learning: A Meta-Analysis and Review of Online Learning Studies." U.S. Department of Education, 2010. http://www2.ed.gov/rschstat/eval/tech/evidence-based-practices /finalreport.pdf

Menchaca, M., and Bekele, T. "Learner and Instructor Identified Success Factors in Distance Education." *Distance Education*, 2008, *29*, 231–252.

Peabody, Z. "College Education Online: Pass? Fail?" *Los Angeles Times*, Sept. 21, 2001. http://articles.latimes.com/2001/sep/27/news/tt-50356

Richardson, J. C., and Swan, K. P. "An Examination of Social Presence in Online Courses in Relation to Students' Perceived Learning and Satisfaction." *Journal of Asynchronous Learning*, 2003, *7*, 68–88.

Rodriguez, M., Ooms, A., and Montañez, M. "Students' Perceptions of Online-Learning Quality Given Comfort, Motivation, Satisfaction, and Experience." *Journal of Interactive Online Learning*, 2008, *7*, 105–125.

Sadera, W. A., Robertson, J., Song, L., and Midon, M. N. "The Role of Community in Online Learning Success." *MERLOT Journal of Online Learning and Teaching*, 2009, *5*(2), 277–284.

Smart, K. L., and Cappel, J. J. "Students' Perceptions of Online Learning: A Comparative Study." *Journal of Information Technology Education*, 2006, *5*, 201–219.

Somenarain, L., Akkaraju, S., and Gharbaran, R. "Student Perceptions and Learning Outcomes in Asynchronous and Synchronous Online Learning Environments in a Biology Course." *MERLOT Journal of Online Learning and Teaching*, 2010, *6*, 353–356.

Song, L., Singleton, E., Hill, J., and Koh, M. "Improving Online Learning: Student Perceptions of Useful and Challenging Characteristics." *Internet and Higher Education*, 2004, *7*, 59–70.

Stewart, C., Bachman, C., and Johnson, R. "Predictors of Faculty Acceptance of Online Education." *MERLOT Journal of Online Learning and Teaching*, 2010, *6*, 597–616.

Vesely, P., Bloom, L., and Sherlock, J. "Key Elements of Building Online Community: Comparing Faculty and Student Perceptions." *MERLOT Journal of Online Learning and Teaching,* 2007, *3,* 234–246.

WCET. "Are Your Online Students Really the Ones Registered for the Course? Student Authentication Requirements for Distance Education Providers." http://wcet.wiche .edu/wcet/docs/publications/Briefing_Paper_Feb_2008.pdf

EDWARD H. PERRY is a professor of mechanical engineering at the University of Memphis and a coeditor of the MERLOT Journal of Online Learning and Teaching.

MICHELLE L. PILATI is a professor of psychology at Rio Hondo College and a coeditor of the MERLOT Journal of Online Learning and Teaching.

NEW DIRECTIONS FOR TEACHING AND LEARNING • DOI: 10.1002/tl

11

This chapter briefly summarizes what has been learned about evidence-based teaching in the preceding chapters and calls for renewed emphasis on preparing teachers to teach well and conduct empirical pedagogical research.

Evidence-Based Teaching: Now and in the Future

William Buskist, James E. Groccia

Our goal in assembling this *New Directions in Teaching and Learning* volume was to introduce college and university teachers to a broad range of approaches that reflect evidence-based teaching (EBT). Our hope, of course, is that we have accomplished this goal and that faculty members will immediately see the inherent benefits of these approaches and, where applicable, adopt one or more of them, or particular aspects of them, in their teaching. After all, as each of the preceding chapters has shown, EBT not only can increase student learning across a variety of measures, it also can increase student engagement in, and enjoyment of, learning. Pedagogical practices that result in high levels of student learning and enjoyment of learning are hallmarks of excellent teaching (Bain, 2004; Buskist, Sikorski, Buckley, and Saville, 2002). In addition, EBT formats, processes, and outcomes clearly align with Chickering and Gamson's (1987) seven principles for good educational practice. Explicitly, these examples of EBT:

1. Enhance contact between students and faculty.
2. Encourage reciprocity and cooperation among students.
3. Emphasize active learning.
4. Offer prompt feedback.
5. Stress time on task.

Implicitly, these EBT systems:

6. Convey high expectations for students' performance.
7. Accommodate diverse talents and approaches to learning.

NEW DIRECTIONS FOR TEACHING AND LEARNING, no. 128, Winter 2011 © Wiley Periodicals, Inc.
Published online in Wiley Online Library (wileyonlinelibrary.com) • DOI: 10.1002/tl.473

Our mission in this chapter is twofold. First, we offer a simple comparative analysis of EBT systems described in this volume in the attempt to summarize what our chapter authors have taught us about EBT. Second, we explore the future of EBT.

Lessons Learned

Our authors' combined efforts permit us the opportunity to step back and form something of a gestalt of EBT. As in all fields, though, it is impossible to reduce the whole of EBT to a simple summation of its components. Nonetheless, given what our authors have discussed regarding the structure and functions of different EBT practices and their attendant outcomes, it is apparent that all EBT systems share at least three common themes.

First, there is no one approach to EBT that is, at this point, superior to another in terms of either its sophistication or structure and its effect on student learning outcomes. All of the EBT systems reviewed in this volume clearly produce favorable student outcomes, although the nature of those outcomes varies from system to system. Indeed, depending on one's context for teaching in combination with one's goals for and conceptions of teaching and learning, different EBT formats may be more or less applicable to one's teaching. Table 1 provides an overview of each of the nine systems of EBT and learning presented in this volume. Even a quick glance at this table reveals that EBT does not exist in a singular, simplified, unified form. Rather, as this volume attests, EBT exists in many formats and can be implemented online, in the classroom, or in hybridized formats. EBT can involve a range of preclass, in-class, and out-of-class activities, or their combination. EBT can accommodate all varieties of student assessment and assess for the entire gamut of cognitive skills found in Bloom's taxonomy (Anderson and others, 2001; Bloom and Krathwohl, 1956).

Second, although their methods differ, all forms of EBT presented in this volume require students to do something—to engage themselves in some activity that demands that they spend time on task discussing, debating, writing about, or otherwise applying the subject matter regardless of what that topic may be. In other words, and as noted, all forms of EBT, including the modernized lecture as described by Chaudhury earlier in this volume, involve active learning. The middle column of Table 1 shows the different ways that each EBT system incorporates active learning into its infrastructure. In reviewing this column, keep in mind that each of these active learning techniques may be borrowed from its respective EBT system and "smuggled" into just about any kind of college and university class as stand-alone exercises regardless of subject matter. For example, one does not need to adopt interteaching in one's instructional practice in order to use prep guides to benefit student learning (and to benefit one's awareness of students' depth of content knowledge). Likewise, one need not adopt the Web-based computer-aided personalized system of instruction as discussed

Table 1. Comparison of Nine Different Systems of Evidence-Based Teaching and Learning

System	General Features and Active Learning Components	Evidence-Based Student Results
Modernized Lecture	Teacher delivers information to groups of students; heavy emphasis on listening and note-taking; may be supplemented with in-class active learning exercises	When used with active learning exercises: enhanced student engagement; long-term retention of knowledge; increased complex thinking skills
Problem-Based Learning	Students work in collaborative groups to solve complex problems developed by the teacher; in-class discussion and debate; teachers often require written answers to problems	Increased retention of content knowledge enhanced teamwork, communication, and problem-solving skills; enhanced student engagement; development of self-regulated learning skills; improved attitudes toward learning
Case Study Teaching	Teacher-led story-based lecture; teacher-facilitated whole class story-based discussions; small group story-based discussion; individual students work on story-based cases	Increased critical-thinking skills, enhanced perspective taking; deeper conceptual understanding; enhanced student engagement
Team-Based Learning	Purposely selected, permanent student teams; individual and team testing for concept mastery; most class time used for applied problem-solving activities; peer evaluation/feedback to promote member accountability to teams	Increased content knowledge; increased retention of knowledge; increased student engagement; positive student attitudes toward group work; increased co-regulation of learning
Interteaching	Students complete "prep" guides before class; student-paired in-class discussion; teacher provides brief, clarifying lectures; interdependent learning with points; frequent in-class assessment	Increased content knowledge; high levels of course preparation; increased motivation; increased levels of self-reported critical thinking
Just-in-Time Teaching	Students answer preclass questions via the Web just prior to class; teacher prepares lecture/lesson based on student answers and facilitates interactive class discussion	Increased content knowledge; increased class attendance; enhanced student preparation for class; improved classroom atmosphere *(continued)*

Table 1. (*Continued*)

System	General Features and Active Learning Components	Evidence-Based Student Results
Service-Learning	Students undertake service activities in collaboration with community members and organizations; students reflect critically on those experiences relative to course content; students receive credit for learning, not for service; nature of student experience dependent on learning and service goals	Increased content knowledge; adoption of (multi-)disciplinary perspectives; increased civic learning and personal and professional development; enhanced critical-thinking/problem-solving skills; increased development of capacity for knowledge production
Web-based Computer-Aided Personalized System of Instruction	Students complete small unit sequential assignments and mastery assessments via the Web and receive immediate feedback; successful students provide feedback to other students through peer-review; students restudy and repeat unsuccessful unit tests; students may also participate in a built-in appeals process	Increased content knowledge and writing skills; enhanced higher-order thinking skills; enhanced enjoyment of learning
Online-Learning	Teacher provides instructional material, including assessment, online in various formats depending on teacher's course goals and student learning outcomes; online teaching may be combined with in-class instruction	Enhanced convenience and flexibility for student learning; increased content knowledge with hybrid courses being especially effective

Note: The precise features and their particular combination may vary within any EBT system of teaching and learning depending on the context of teaching and the course goals that teachers establish for their specific courses.

by Pear and others earlier in this volume in order to incorporate mastery-based learning in one's classes.

Third, adopting and implementing any given EBT system will require advance planning and considerable time investment on the part of the teacher. But then any form of good teaching demands thought, time, and effort from the teacher (Svinicki and McKeachie, 2011). The advantage of adopting and implementing a given EBT system, of course, is that its effectiveness as a teaching tool has been empirically validated. Although no EBT system is foolproof or so easy that "even a caveman could do it," if one follows the detailed implementation instructions given for any of the EBT systems described in this volume, there is a reasonable chance that one's teaching will produce, or at least approximate, the corresponding learning outcomes (see Table 1, right-hand column).

Future of EBT

As this volume clearly demonstrates, researchers in higher education have enthusiastically answered Boyer's (1990) clarion call for broader and deeper scholarship on teaching and learning by creatively developing and empirically testing an array of pedagogical systems aimed at improving student learning. To be sure, ample data now exist to support unequivocally the claim that college and university teachers can enhance student learning— from the simple learning of content to the more arduous learning of analytical and critical thought—by employing specific evidence-based tactics in their teaching.

That is the good news. The bad news is that not all college and university teachers practice EBT. Just as some medical doctors fail to stay current with cutting-edge research in their specialty areas, some teachers do not stay current with cutting-edge approaches in teaching their subject matter. However, the problem in teaching is much worse than merely staying updated. Unlike medical doctors, who all have received training—and very likely intense training—to practice medicine, many teachers have not had any training whatsoever in teaching (Boice, 2000).

If there is to be a future for EBT or, for that matter, a future for any effective teaching practice, there must be mechanisms in place to inform faculty members of all ranks and disciplines about it in terms of both its proper implementation and its usefulness in enhancing student learning. Fortunately, many colleges and universities have recognized the need for the proper preparation of teachers. Many academic departments offer workshops, seminars, and classes for graduate students interested in teaching careers, and many institutions have established "teaching and learning" centers to assist faculty members (and graduate students) in developing and refining their teaching skills. In the United States, however, such offerings at both departmental and institutional levels are voluntary, and only a minority of graduate students and faculty members participate in teaching development activities. As a result, many teachers are likely unaware of EBT as well as the wider assortment of practices involved in teaching well.

Thus, departmental teaching leaders and supervisors and teaching and learning center directors must continue to press forward with both stressing the need for appropriate preparation and training for college and university teachers and routinely sponsoring activities that introduce faculty members and graduate students to EBT. But these developers of teachers should not stop there. Training faculty members and graduate students to implement EBT practices is not sufficient to guarantee EBT's longevity.

NEW DIRECTIONS FOR TEACHING AND LEARNING • DOI: 10.1002/tl

Accomplishing this feat first requires preparing the institutional culture to prize, accept, nurture, and sustain an environment that promotes EBT. Academic traditions at the heart of the research endeavor must transfer to the classroom so that a scholarly ethos prevails where it becomes part of the collective institutional and individual identity of each teacher to teach in a way that is based on, and consistent with, an empirical approach (McDaniel and Wooldridge, forthcoming). Without such a culture, efforts to implement the EBT systems described in this volume may not be rewarded and may be difficult to initiate and sustain over time.

Within this welcoming academic culture, acts of procreation, which in this case means continued research into EBT in order to understand and refine existing practices and to create new ones, must occur. In other words, the future of EBT rests not only in teaching and supporting teachers to practice EBT but in also teaching and supporting teachers to engage in the scholarship of teaching and learning with respect to it (Gurung and Schwartz, 2009).

As teachers, we are fortunate to work in a natural laboratory setting: The classroom is not only an environment for instruction, it is also an environment that lends itself well to applied research on a vast array of teaching practices, on their myriad permutations, and on their effects on student affect, motivation, and learning. Hence, any teacher who aspires to conduct empirical research into teaching and learning has the perfect setting for doing so.

The question, of course, is: What issues should such research address? The answer is another question, albeit simple one, although the steps required in answering it may be complex: Will EBT enhance the effectiveness of one's teaching (with "effectiveness" defined as favorably impacting a salient aspect of student learning)? Hence, one could start by merely investigating whether any one of the EBT systems delineated in this volume "works" in one's classroom. Or perhaps one might rather recombine different elements within an EBT system, or even between EBT systems, in a novel way to explore their effects on student learning, thereby creating an entirely novel EBT system.

We must also remember that EBT is not restricted to enclosed and well-defined systems of teaching and learning that span an entire academic term. EBT also exists in more limited formats that can be used in the short term: a demonstration, role play, video, and other class activities that can be used to enhance some aspect of student learning. Empirical data on the effectiveness of such activities relative to improved student learning is valuable in its own right and would be of interest to one's colleagues. Thus, in the broadest sense, EBT should be conceptualized as any empirically validated instructional activity or set of activities, regardless of duration, that improves student learning.

Cast in this light, there are many different research questions about EBT that could be addressed. When one considers the different contexts in which teaching and learning occur—small classes and large classes, on-campus and off-campus classes, online and hybrid classes, low-level and high-level classes, and so on—the number of research questions probably borders on infinity. As long as such questions exist and teachers are interested and prepared properly to answer them, EBT will enjoy what would seem to be an eternal future.

References

Anderson, L. W., and others (eds.). *A Taxonomy for Learning, Teaching, and Assessing: A Revision of Bloom's Taxonomy of Educational Objectives.* Boston: Allyn and Bacon, 2001.

Bain, K. *What the Best College Teachers Do.* Cambridge, Mass.: Harvard University Press, 2004.

Bloom, B. S., and Krathwohl, D. R. *Taxonomy of Educational Objectives: The Classification of Educational Goals by a Committee of College and University Examiners. Handbook I: Cognitive Domain.* New York: Longmans, Green, 1956.

Boice, R. *Advice for New Faculty Members: Nihil Nimus.* Needham Heights, Mass.: Allyn and Bacon, 2000.

Boyer, E. L. *Scholarship Reconsidered: Priorities of the Professoriate.* New York: Carnegie Foundation for the Advancement of Teaching, 1990.

Buskist, W., Sikorski, J., Buckley, T., and Saville, B. K. "Elements of Master Teaching." In S. F. Davis and W. Buskist (eds.), *The Teaching of Psychology: Essays in Honor of Wilbert J. McKeachie and Charles L. Brewer* (pp. 27–39). Mahwah, N.J.: Lawrence Erlbaum, 2002.

Chickering, A. W., and Gamson, Z. F. "Seven Principles for Good Practice in Undergraduate Education." *AAHE Bulletin,* 1987, *39*(7), 3–7.

Gurung, R.A.R., and Schwartz, B. M. *Optimizing Teaching and Learning: Practicing Pedagogical Research.* Malden, Mass.: Wiley-Blackwell, 2009.

McDaniel, M. A., and Wooldridge, C. "The Science of Learning and Its Applications." In W. Buskist and V. Benassi (eds.), *Effective College and University Teaching: Strategies and Tactics for the New Professoriate.* Thousand Oaks, Calif.: Sage, forthcoming.

Svinicki, M., and McKeachie, W. J. *McKeachie's Teaching Tips: Strategies, Research, and Theory for College and University Teachers.* (13th ed.) Belmont, Calif.: Wadsworth, 2011.

WILLIAM BUSKIST *is the distinguished professor of the teaching of psychology and a faculty fellow at the Biggio Center for the Enhancement of Teaching and Learning at Auburn University.*

JAMES E. GROCCIA *is director of the Biggio Center for the Enhancement of Teaching and Learning and associate professor of Higher Education at Auburn University.*

NEW DIRECTIONS FOR TEACHING AND LEARNING • DOI: 10.1002/tl

INDEX

Abdel-Salam, T. M., 97
Abes, E. S., 81
Africa, 96
Ahlfeldt, S., 26
Akkaraju, S., 100
Alaimo, P. J., 24
Albanese, M. S., 22–23
Allen, D. E., 21, 23, 34
Allen, I. E., 95, 100
Amador, J. A., 23
Ambrose, S. A., 8
American Association of Colleges and Universities, 6
American Association of Physics Teachers, 13
American Journal of Distance Education, 96
American Psychological Association, 7–8
Anderson, L. W., 106
Anderson, P., 26
Anderton, J. B., 53
Angelino, L., 100
Anson, C., 26
APA style. *See Publication Manual of the American Psychological Association (APA style)*
Arons, A. B., 67, 70
Ash, S. L., 77, 78, 80, 82
Asoko, H. M., 65
Association of American Colleges and Universities, 78
Astin, A. W., 65, 79–81
Atkinson, M. P., 80
Audience response systems, 34. *See also* Clicker technology
Axe, J. B., 59

Bachman, C., 101
Baer, D. M., 54
Bain, K., 1, 105
Bangert-Drowns, R. L., 85
Baron, J., 99
Barrows, H., 21, 32
Baxter Magolda, M. B., 67
Bean, J. C., 24
Beatty, S. J., 50
Beder, H., 5
Beghetto, R. A., 65
Beichner, R., 16, 17
Bekele, T., 98
Benedict, J. O., 53

Benjamin, L. T., Jr., 53
Bergland, M., 33
Berners-Lee, T., 95
Bernhardt, S. A., 21, 34
Best Evidence Encyclopedia, 6
Biesta, G., 8
BlackBerry, 87
Blackboard, 85
Blake, B., 67
Blake, R. L., 22–23
Blended instruction, 97
Bligh, D. A., 14, 18
Bloom, B. S., 67, 80, 87, 106
Bloom, L., 98
Bloom's taxonomy, 67, 80, 87
Blumberg, P., 26
Boehr, B. J., 90
Boice, R., 109
Bok, D. C., 6, 7
Borges, N. J., 50
Boud, D. J., 21
Boyce, T. E., 55–57
Boyer, E. L., 1, 75, 109
Boyer Commission on EducatingUndergraduates in the Research University, 6
Brandenberger, J., 80
Bransford, J. D., 8, 15, 41, 65, 67
Bray, C., 50
Bringle, R., 75, 76
Broadwell, M. M., 14
Brown, A. L., 8, 15, 41, 65
Brown, M., 101
Bruff, D., 17
Bubier, J. L., 25
Bucket theory, 21–22
Buckley, T., 105
Burnett, R. E., 24
Buskist, W., 5, 54, 105
Butler, A., 25, 26

California Critical Thinking Disposition Inventory, 25
Cambell Collaboration (Norway), 6
Cannella-Malone, H. L., 59
Cappel, J. J., 100
CAPSI. *See* Computer-aided personalized system of instruction
Carini, R. M., 78
Carmichael, K., 54
Carnegie Foundation, 75

Case It!, 34, 37; Investigator, 34; Launch Pad, 34; Simulator, 34
Case study teaching, 31–38, 107; and case studies and cone of learning, 36–38; and case study methods, 31–34; and clicker cases, 34; and computer simulation cases, 33–34; and discussion methods, 32; and individual cases, 33; and lecture method, 32; review of empirical evidence for, 34–36; and small-group methods, 32–33
Chaudhury, S. R., 13, 36, 53, 106
Chickering, A. W., 98, 105
Chinn, C. A., 23
Chudowski, N., 16
Clark, M. C., 50
Clayton, P. H., 75, 77, 78, 80, 82
Clicker cases, 34, 37
Clicker technology, 17, 18
Cliff, W., 33
Cocking, R. R., 8, 15, 41, 65
Cohen, P. A., 53, 85
Colby, A., 75
Cole, R., 6
Comprehensive School Reform Quality Center, 6
Computer simulation cases, 33–34
Computer-aided personalized system of instruction (CAPSI), 86–89; and accuracy and quality of peer feedback, 90; comparisons of, with other teaching methods, 89; and correlates of success in CAPSI course, 89–90; and future research, 91; and higher order thinking, 90; operating characteristics of, 89; and peer reviewing, 90–91; and procrastination, 90; psychological and educational underpinnings and connections of, 87–88; research studies, 89–91
Conant, J., 31, 32
Cone of Learning, 36–38
Cooper, J. O., 54
Cranton, P., 82
Crone-Todd, D. E., 86, 87, 89, 90
Crooks, S. M., 99
Crossman, G. R., 97
Crouch, C. H., 16, 70
Culley, M. R., 25
Cush, D., 54

Dale, E., 36
Darby, A., 81

Davidson, D., 25
Davis, B. G., 14
DeAngelo, L., 9, 10
"Decisions, Decisions," 49
DeGrandpre, R. J., 54
Dennick, R., 14
DeShields, O. W., Jr., 88
Desire2Learn, 85
Devine, S., 90
Dewey, J., 76, 81
Di Leonardi, B., 14
Discussion methods, 32
Dochy, F., 22, 34, 53
Donham, R. S., 21, 34
Donnelly, M. B., 23
Donovan, S. S., 25
Doscher, S., 50
Dow, M., 100
Downing, K., 25
Drabick, D.A.G., 25
Driver, R. H., 65
Duch, B. J., 21, 23, 24
Duncan, D., 17
Duncan, R. G., 23
DuRei, K., 33

Easley, J. L., 70
Eatkin, R., 32
EBT. See Evidence-based teaching
Educating Citizens: Preparing America's Undergraduates for Lives of Moral and Civic Responsibility (Colby and others), 75
Ehrlich, T., 76
Ehrmann, S. C., 98
Elder, L., 80
Elliott, K. M., 88
Elliott, M. P., 57
Engle, C. E., 22
Espiritu, R., 8
European Organization for Nuclear Research, 95
Evidence Based Teaching (Petty), 41
Evidence for Policy and Practice Information and Co-ordination Center (United Kingdom), 6
Evidence-based teaching: and case-study teaching, 31–38, 107; comparison of nine different systems of, 107–108; and current status of higher education, 5–7; future of, 109–111; and interteaching, 53–59, 107; and just-in-time teaching, 63–72, 107; modernized lecture system of, 13–19,

107; nature of, and implications for teaching and learning, 7–10; need for, 5–10; and online learning, 95–102, 108; and problem-based learning system, 21–27, 107; and service learning, 75–82, 105; and seven evidence-based principles of learning, 8–9; six best practices in, 41; and Team-based learning, 41–50, 107; and Web-based computer-aided personalized system of instruction, 85–92, 108
Exley, K., 14
Eyler, J., 77, 79, 80, 82

Fagen, A. P., 16
FCI. *See* Force Concept Inventory
Felten, P., 75, 81
Fink, L., 33, 41
Fitch, P., 81
Force Concept Inventory (FCI), 24–25, 70
Formica, S. P., 70
Franklin, B., 63
Friedman, T., 6

Games, R., 75
Gamson, Z. F., 105
Gavrin, A., 67, 71
GeoBytes, 64
Gharbaran, R., 100
Gijbels, D., 22, 34, 53
Gilchrist, L. Z., 81
Giles, D. E., Jr., 80, 82
Glaser, R., 16
Gonyea, R., 26
Goto, K., 58
Gray, C. J., 80
Gray, J. A., 7
Groccia, J. E., 5, 6, 105
Groh, S. E., 21, 23
Guertin, L. A., 64, 71
Gurung, R.A.R., 1, 110

Haber, J., 8
Hake, R., 16, 18, 24, 35, 70
Hakel, M., 16, 53
Halloun, I., 70
Halpern, D., 16, 53
Hammer, D., 18
Handelsman, J., 18, 19
Hartley, M., 75, 82
Harvard Business School, 31
Hastings, T., 87
Hatcher, J., 76

Hattie, J., 41
Haynes, R. B., 7
Heron, T. E., 54
Herreid, C. F., 31–34
Hestenes, D., 70
Heward, W. L., 54
Higher education, current status of, 5–7
Higher Education Research Institute (University of California, Los Angeles), 9
High-Impact Educational Practices (Kuh), 78
Hill, J., 100
Hineline, P. N., 55–57
Hmelo-Silver, C. E., 23
Hoffman, E. S., 100
"How Civic Engagement is Reframing Liberal Education" (Rhoads), 75
How People Learn: Brain, Mind, Experience, and School (Bransford and others), 67
Howard, J., 77
Hung, W., 23
Hybrid instruction, 97

Ikeda, E. K., 79
Immediate Feedback Assessment Technique (IF-AT), 43, 44
Indiana University, 63
Indiana University-Purdue University at Indianapolis (IUPUI), 67, 68, 70–71
Individual readiness assurance test (iRAT), 43
International Journal for the Scholarship of Teaching and Learning, 1
International Research Conference on Service-Learning and Community Engagement, 76
Interteaching, 53–59, 107; and behavior analysis and education, 54–55; and capitalizing on established learning principles, 56–57; components of, 55; research on, 57–59
iPhone, 87
iRAT. *See* Individual readiness assurance test (iRAT)

Jaeger, A., 82
James, W., 1
Jameson, J., 80, 82
JiTT. *See* Just-in-Time Teaching (JiTT)
Johnson, D. W., 24–26, 32
Johnson, R., 101
Johnson, R. T., 24–26, 32

JOLT. *See Journal of Online Learning and Teaching* (JOLT)

Jonassen, D. H., 23

Jones, S. R., 81

Journal of Asynchronous Learning Networks, 96

Journal of Distance Education, 96

Journal of Educators Online, 96

Journal of Interactive Online Learning, 96

Journal of Online Learning and Teaching (JOLT), 96

Just-in-time teaching (JiTT), 63–72, 107; adapting, to one's teaching style, 68–69; basics of, 64–65; and classroom climate, motivation, and attitude, 70–71; and cognitive gains, 70; demands of, on students, 69; developing lesson in, 66–67; making difference in student learning with, 69–70; successful implementation of, 65–68

Kahne, J., 81

Kang, H., 35, 37

Kang, K., 35, 37

Kara, A., 88

Karplus, R., 15

Kauffmann, P. J., 97

Kay, R., 35

Kaynak, E., 88

Kazdin, A. E., 8

Keller, F. S., 1, 2, 54–55, 85

Khoo, H. E., 22

Kim, H., 64

Kim, S., 35

King, M. P., 46

Kinsner, W., 86, 89

Klein, P. D., 24

Klein, S. P., 78

Kleinman, S., 97

Kline, M., 6

Knight, A., 33

Knight, A. B., 41

Knight, J. K., 17

Koh, D., 22

Koh, G. C.-H., 22

Koh, M., 100

Koles, P. G., 50

Krathwohl, D. R., 106

Kuh, G. D., 78, 79

Kulik, C., 53, 85

Kulik, J. A., 53, 85

Lai, P., 25, 53

Lambert, J., 55, 85, 90

Langenhan, J. M., 24

Laws, P., 16

Leacock, S., 13

Learning cycle approach (lecturing), 15

LeClair, R. J., 48

Lecturing, 13–19; applying learning sciences research to, 15–16; learning cycle approach to, 15; method, 32; methods and systems for, 14–15; modernized, 107; student attitude toward, 18

LeSage, A., 35

Levine, R. E., 41, 50

Light, R. J., 26

Liu, R., 23

LoBiondo-Wood, G., 8

Lord, T., 36

Lowman, J., 1

Lundeberg, M., 35, 37

Lundy, B. L., 81

Madaus, G., 87

Maier, M., 64, 65, 70, 71

Malloy, E. A., 75

Malott, R. W., 54

Manyan, D. R., 48

Marrs, K., 68, 70, 71

Martin, G., 88, 90, 91

Martin, T. L., 89–91

Maryland Physics Expectations Survey (MPEX), 18

Marzano, R. J., 41

Mayer, R. E., 17

Mayo, W. P., 23

Mazur, E., 16, 70

McClure, J. D., 82

McDaniel, M. A., 110

McInnerney, J. M., 100

McIntosh, R., 76

McKeachie, W. J., 14, 36, 37, 108

McLeish, J., 14

McMahon, K. K., 41

McMaster University (Canada), 31

Means, B., 101

Medina, P., 5

Mehta, S., 26

Menchaca, M., 98

MERLOT (Multimedia Resource for Learning and Online Teaching), 95–96

Metz, A.J.R., 8

Mezirow, J., 82

Michael, J., 56

Michaelsen, L. K., 33, 41, 50, 87
Michigan Journal for Community Service Learning, 76
Middendorf, J., 67
Middendorf-Pace Decoding the Disciplines Cycle Inventory, 67
Midon, M. N., 98
Miles, L., 23
Miller, S., 19
Mitchell, S., 22–23
Montañez, M., 100
Moodle, 85
Moore, K. A., 8
Moran, D. J., 54
Morgan, K., 37
Morrill Act (1862), 75
Mosaic (Web browser), 95
MPEX. *See* Maryland Physics Expectations Survey (MPEX)
Mpofu, E., 79
Murray, J., 26
Myers, A. C., 25

Nandi, P. L., 22
National Center for Education Statistics, 7
National Center for Public Policy on Higher Education (NCPPHE), 7
National Research Council (NRC), 15, 16
National Science Digital Library (NSDL), 95–96
National Study of Student Engagement (NSSE), 26, 78, 79
Natvig, D., 100
NCPPHE. *See* National Center for Public Policy on Higher Education (NCPPHE)
Nelson, S., 50
Newman, M., 24
Newtonian thinking skills, 70
Nguyen, H. T., 50
Nichols, L., 21, 24
No Child Left Behind, 6
North Georgia College and State University, 70
Novak, G. M., 63
Novak, M., 89, 90
NRC. *See* National Research Council (NRC)
NSDL. *See* National Science Digital Library (NSDL)
NSSE. *See* National Study of Student Engagement (NSSE)

Onion, R., 47
Online Journal of Distance Learning Administration, 96
Online Learning, 95–102, 108; empirical evidence regarding, 99–102; evidence of effectiveness of, 101–102; and faculty perceptions, 100–101; implementation of, 97–99; and student perceptions, 99–100
Ooms, A., 100

Pace, D., 63, 64, 67–69
Paine, C., 26
Paper Chase, The (movie), 32
Parker, E. D., 59
Parmelee, D. X., 41, 50
Pascarella, E. T., 58, 80, 81
Pascual-Leone, A., 38
Patry, M., 35
Paul, L., 25
Paul, R., 80
PBL. *See* Problem-based learning (PBL)
PBL Clearinghouse, 23
Peabody, Z., 101
Pear, J. J., 85–91
Pearce, D., 25
Peer instruction (PI), 16
Peer-Reviewer Training Manual (PRTM; Schnerch, Devine, and Pear), 90
Pelaez, N. J., 24–25
Pellegrino, J. W., 16
Pelton-Sweet, L. M., 44
Perry, E. J., 95
Personalized system of instruction (PSI), 1–2, 54, 55, 85, 86
Personalized system of instruction (PSI), Web-based computer-aided. *See* Web-based computer-aided personalized system of instruction
Peters, C. B., 23
Petty, G., 5, 41, 43, 46, 48
Pfund, C., 19
Phillmann, K.-B., 25
PI. *See* Peer instruction (PI)
Piaget, J., 15
Pilatti, M. L., 95
PowerPoint, 34, 37
Pribbenow, C. M., 19
Problem-based learning (PBL), 21–27, 107; effectiveness of, on content learning in undergraduate settings, 24–25; effectiveness of, on process

skills, 25; effectiveness of, on student engagement, 25–26; origins of, in medical schools, 21–23; strategies for implementation of, 23–24
Project on Student Debt, 7
PSI. *See* Personalized system of instruction (PSI)
Publication Manual of the American Psychological Association (APA style), 88, 89

Questioning, technique of, 17

Read, C. N., 87
Readiness assurance process (RAP), 43–45
Redish, E. F., 18
Respet, A. J., 82
Restad, P., 47
Reynolds, A., 47
Rhoads, R., 75
Richardson, J. C., 100
Richardson, W. S., 7
Rischard, J. F., 6
Risley, T. R., 54
Roberts, T. S., 100
Robertson, J., 55, 98
Rodriguez, M., 100
Roopa, R., 50
Rosenberg, W. M., 7
Rumsfeld, D., 65

Sackett, D. L., 7
Sadera, W. A., 98
Saltmarsh, J., 75, 82
Saul, J. M., 18
Saville, B. K., 53, 55, 57, 58, 105
SCALE-UP. *See* Student-Centered Activities for Large Enrollment Undergraduate Programs (SCALE-UP)
Schneider, J., 58
Schnerch, G. J., 85, 90
Scholarship of teaching and learning movement (SoTL), 1
Scholarship Reconsidered (Boyer), 1
Schwartz, B. M., 1, 110
Schwartz, R. W., 23
Scoboria, A., 58
Scott, P. H., 65, 69
Seaman, J., 95, 100
Segers, M., 22, 34, 53
Sellnow, T., 26
"Serviced-Learning: Three Principles" (Sigmon), 76

Service-learning, 75–82, 105; conceptual framework for, 78; defining, designing, and implementing, 76–77; review of empirical evidence regarding, 77–81; transformative potential of, 81–82
Shankar, N., 50
Sharp, W., 50
Sheppard, S. D., 25–26
Sherin, N., 13
Sherlock, J., 98
Sherman, J. G., 86
Shin, D., 88
Sigmon, R., 76
Sikorski, J., 105
Silva, K. M., 85, 90
Silverman, R., 24
Simister, H., 87
Simkins, S., 64, 65, 70, 71
Sinclair, M., 50
Singleton, E., 100
Skinner, B. F., 54, 85
Slavin, R. E., 5, 6
Sloan-C (Sloan Consortium), 95–96
Small-group methods, 32–33
Smart, K. L., 100
Smart, L., 25
Smith, K. A., 24–26, 32
Snow, C. E., 67
So, M., 25, 53
Socratic dialogue, 31
Sokoloff, D., 18
Somenarain, L., 100
Song, L., 98, 100
SoTL. *See* Scholarship of teaching and learning movement (SoTL)
South America, 96
Spraker, M. C., 70
Springer, C. R., 90
Springer, L., 25
Stanne, M. E., 25
Steinberg, R. N., 18
Stenson, C. M., 80
Stewart, C., 101
Stewart, T. L., 25, 81
Stolfi, A., 50
Strage, A. A., 79
Student-Centered Activities for Large Enrollment Undergraduate Programs (SCALE-UP), 16, 17
Substantive conflict, 24
Summerlee, A., 26
Svenningsen, L., 85, 89
Svinicki, M., 14, 37, 108

Swan, K. P., 100
Sweet, M., 41, 44, 47, 87

Tamblyn, R., 21, 32
TBL. *See* Team-based learning (TBL)
Teaching, faculty approaches to, 10
Team readiness assurance test (tRAT), 43, 44
Team-based learning (TBL), 41–50, 107; and 4-S application activities, 45–47; argument template example for, 47; evidence for effectiveness of, 49–50; feedback form (sample), 49; four essential elements of, 42–49; four practical elements of, 41; and peer evaluation, 48–49; and readiness assurance, 43–45; representative concept map generated by, 48; and strategically formed, permanent teams, 42–43; and typical TBL unit, 42
Team-Based Learning clearinghouse, 50
Terenzini, P. T., 80, 81
Texas Tech University, 67
Thompson, K. H., 48
Thorndike, E. L., 54, 56
Thornton, R., 18
Tinto, V., 26
Tiwari, A., 25, 53
tRAT. *See* Team readiness assurance test (tRAT)

Udovic, D., 16
United States Medical Licensing Examination (USMLE), 22
University of California, Berkeley, 32
University of California, Los Angeles, 9
University of Delaware, 21, 23
University of Illinois, 95
University of Manitoba (Canada), 86–87, 89
U.S. Air Force Academy, 70
U.S. Department of Defense, 95
U.S. Department of Education, 101
USMLE. *See* United States Medical Licensing Examination (USMLE)

Van den Bossche, P., 22, 34, 53
Vandenberg, B., 82
Vernon, D.T.A., 22–23

Veseley, P., 98
Visions of the Future: A History (Pace; course), 63
Vogelsang, L. J., 79

Watson, W. E., 50
WCET. *See* WICHE Cooperative for Technical Education
Web-based computer-aided personalized system of instruction (WebCAPSI), 85–92, 108; background to, 85–87; benefits of, 88–89; benefits of, to department and university, 88; benefits of, to students, 89; benefits of, to teachers, 88–89
WebCT, 85
Weisberg, R., 25
Welty, W. H., 24
Westheimer, J., 81
What Works Clearinghouse, 6
Whitney, B. C., 82
WICHE Cooperative for Technical Education (WCET), 98
Williams, B. A., 24
Williams, F., 100
Wilson, J. M., 16
Wilson, W. R., 50
Winterson, B. J., 48
Wirth, K., 87
Wolf, M. M., 54
Wolter, B.H.K., 35, 37
Wong, M. L., 22
Wood, E. J., 21, 22
Wood, W. B., 17
Woods, D., 23
Wooldridge, C., 110
World Wide Web, 95
Wright, A., 33
Wright State University, 50
Wurr, A. J., 79

Yadav, A., 35
Yee, J. A., 179
Yuen, K., 53
Yurn, K., 25

Zappe, S. E., 64
Zinn, T. E., 53, 57, 58
Zollman, D. A., 13–15, 19
Zollman, K., 13, 14

NEW DIRECTIONS FOR TEACHING AND LEARNING
ORDER FORM SUBSCRIPTION AND SINGLE ISSUES

DISCOUNTED BACK ISSUES:

Use this form to receive 20% off all back issues of *New Directions for Teaching and Learning*.
All single issues priced at **$23.20** (normally $29.00)

TITLE	ISSUE NO.	ISBN

Call 888-378-2537 or see mailing instructions below. When calling, mention the promotional code JBNND to receive your discount. For a complete list of issues, please visit www.josseybass.com/go/ndtl

SUBSCRIPTIONS: (1 YEAR, 4 ISSUES)

☐ New Order ☐ Renewal

U.S.	☐ Individual: $89	☐ Institutional: $275
CANADA/MEXICO	☐ Individual: $89	☐ Institutional: $315
ALL OTHERS	☐ Individual: $113	☐ Institutional: $349

Call 888-378-2537 or see mailing and pricing instructions below.
Online subscriptions are available at www.onlinelibrary.wiley.com

ORDER TOTALS:

Issue / Subscription Amount: $ _____

Shipping Amount: $ _____
(for single issues only – subscription prices include shipping)

Total Amount: $ _____

SHIPPING CHARGES:	
First Item	$6.00
Each Add'l Item	$2.00

(No sales tax for U.S. subscriptions. Canadian residents, add GST for subscription orders. Individual rate subscriptions must be paid by personal check or credit card. Individual rate subscriptions may not be resold as library copies.)

BILLING & SHIPPING INFORMATION:

☐ **PAYMENT ENCLOSED:** *(U.S. check or money order only. All payments must be in U.S. dollars.)*

☐ **CREDIT CARD:** ☐ VISA ☐ MC ☐ AMEX

Card number _____ Exp. Date _____

Card Holder Name _____ Card Issue # _____

Signature _____ Day Phone _____

☐ **BILL ME:** *(U.S. institutional orders only. Purchase order required.)*

Purchase order # _____
Federal Tax ID 13559302 • GST 89102-8052

Name _____

Address _____

Phone _____ E-mail _____

Copy or detach page and send to: **John Wiley & Sons, One Montgomery Street, Suite 1200, San Francisco, CA 94104-4594**

Order Form can also be faxed to: **888-481-2665**

PROMO JBNND

Statement of Ownership

Statement of Ownership, Management, and Circulation (required by 39 U.S.C. 3685), filed on OCTOBER 1, 2011 for NEW DIRECTIONS FOR TEACHING AND LEARNING (Publication No. 0271-0633), published Quarterly for an annual subscription price of $89 at Wiley Subscription Services, Inc., at Jossey-Bass, One Montgomery St., Suite 1200, San Francisco, CA 94104-4594.

The names and complete mailing addresses of the Publisher, Editor, and Managing Editor are: Publisher, Wiley Subscription Services, Inc., A Wiley Company at San Francisco, One Montgomery St., Suite 1200, San Francisco, CA 94104-4594; Editor, Catherine M. Wehlburg, TCU Box 297028, Texas Christian University, Fort Worth TX 76129; Managing Editor, None. . Contact Person: Joe Schuman; Telephone: 415-782-3232.

NEW DIRECTIONS FOR TEACHING AND LEARNING is a publication owned by Wiley Subscription Services, Inc., 111 River St., Hoboken, NJ 07030. The known bondholders, mortgagees, and other security holders owning or holding 1% or more of total amount of bonds, mortgages, or other securities are (see list).

	Average No. Copies Each Issue During Preceding 12 Months	No. Copies Of Single Issue Published Nearest To Filing Date (Summer 2011)
15a. Total number of copies (net press run)	1,043	997
15b. Legitimate paid and/or requested distribution (by mail and outside mail)		
15b(1). Individual paid/requested mail subscriptions stated on PS form 3541 (include direct written request from recipient, telemarketing, and Internet requests from recipient, paid subscriptions including nominal rate subscriptions, advertiser's proof copies, and exchange copies)	405	371
15b(2). Copies requested by employers for distribution to employees by name or position, stated on PS form 3541	0	0
15b(3). Sales through dealers and carriers, street vendors, counter sales, and other paid or requested distribution outside USPS	0	0
15b(4). Requested copies distributed by other mail classes through USPS	0	0
15c. Total paid and/or requested circulation (sum of 15b(1), (2), (3), and (4))	405	371
15d. Nonrequested distribution (by mail and outside mail)		
15d(1). Outside county nonrequested copies stated on PS form 3541	14	13
15d(2). In-county nonrequested copies stated on PS form 3541	0	0
15d(3). Nonrequested copies distributed through the USPS by other classes of mail	0	0
15d(4). Nonrequested copies distributed outside the mail	0	0
15e. Total nonrequested distribution (sum of 15d(1), (2), (3), and (4))	14	13
15f. Total distribution (sum of 15c and 15e)	419	384
15g. Copies not distributed	624	613
15h. Total (sum of 15f and 15g)	1,043	997
15i. Percent paid and/or requested circulation (15c divided by 15f times 100)	96.8%	96.6%

I certify that all information furnished on this form is true and complete. I understand that anyone who furnishes false or misleading information on this form or who omits material or information requested on this form may be subject to criminal sanctions (including fines and imprisonment) and/or civil sanctions (including civil penalties).

Statement of Ownership will be printed in the Winter 2011 issue of this publication.

(signed) Susan E. Lewis, VP & Publisher-Periodicals

4811350R00071

Made in the USA
San Bernardino, CA
08 October 2013